THE
SOCIAL SALES
PLAYBOOK

The Social Sales Playbook:
Developing a B2B Sales Plan That Drives Results

© Mark Hillary 2024
All Rights Reserved

Published by Carnaby Books
São Paulo
Brazil

www.carnabysp.com
www.markhillary.com

THE SOCIAL SALES PLAYBOOK

DEVELOPING A B2B SALES PLAN
THAT DRIVES RESULTS

MARK HILLARY

Carnaby Books
São Paulo
Brazil

www.carnabysp.com

Author portrait supplied by the author.

Cover art by: Giovanni Misagrande

ISBN: 979 833 917 5735

The Social Sales Playbook:
Developing a B2B Sales Plan That Drives Results

© Mark Hillary 2024

The right of Mark Hillary to be identified as the author of this work has been asserted by them in accordance with the Copyright, Designs and Patents Act 1988.

All rights reserved. No part of this publication may be reproduced, stored in or introduced into a retrieval system, or transmitted, in any form, or by any means (electronic, mechanical, photocopying, recording, or otherwise) without the prior written permission of the publisher. Any person who does any unauthorized act in relation to this publication may be liable to criminal prosecution and civil claim for damages.

This is for Olivia Orwell Hillary -
my little editor

CONTENTS

Foreword: Thoughts From Paul O'Hara - B2B Sales Expert xiii
Chapter One: Covid Changed Everything 1
Chapter Two: Why Is Social Sales So Important Today? 13
Chapter Three: Target Audience Identification 23
Chapter Four: Building Your Content Strategy 33
Chapter Five: Designing Engagement and Interaction 49
Chapter Six: Personal Branding 61
Chapter Seven: How To Use Social Listening 73
Chapter Eight: Networking and Relationship Building 85
Chapter Nine: Showing The Value Proposition 97
Chapter Ten: Lead Nurturing And Building A Pipeline ... 107
Chapter Eleven: Measurement and Analytics 117
Chapter Twelve: Training and Empowerment 127
Chapter Thirteen: Collaboration with Marketing 137
Chapter Fourteen: Consistency and Persistence 147
Conclusion: Start Simple And Build Over Time 157
Appendix: Driving Into A New Future For B2B Social Sales 167

About The Author

Mark Hillary is one of the best-known global analysts focused on technology and customer experience (CX). Before this book, he has already published another 25 highly influential books on various aspects of technology and has written commentary for the BBC, Reuters, Financial Times, and many trade journals. He is a regular CX commentator in Intelligent Sourcing and Engage Customer magazines.

Mark's books have covered subjects such as artificial intelligence, ChatGPT, business outsourcing, Gig CX, and globalization. His 'Global Services' book was published by the British Computer Society and the United Nations published his social media guide for small businesses.

Mark has also ghosted content for CEOs, sales leaders, political leaders in several countries, and once wrote jokes about the moon to help the astronaut Neil Armstrong improve his speeches.

Mark was the first ever official blogger hired by the British department for education. He was one of the 100 official bloggers covering the London 2012 Olympic Games. He has travelled across Asia and Africa as an adviser to the United

Nations - focused on helping developing nations boost their local tech industry.

Mark has extensive experience teaching MBA students at London South Bank university and his own MBA is from the University of Liverpool.

Mark's weekly podcast 'CX Files', co-hosted with the Canadian CX analyst Peter Ryan, has featured interviews with some of the most important leaders in the customer experience industry. The podcast is one of the most popular shows globally focused on CX and is listed in the top 5% of all available podcasts. The back catalogue now features over 330 interviews.

Mark is British and is based in São Paulo, Brazil. He lives with his wife, daughter, and two Staffordshire Bull Terrier dogs.

www.markhillary.com
bit.ly/markhillarybooks
cxfiles.libsyn.com/cxfiles

FOREWORD

Thoughts From Paul O'Hara - B2B Sales Expert

Throughout my career, I have been deeply entrenched in the world of sales, particularly focused on developing strategies for business-to-business (B2B) sales teams.

Today, I'm privileged to be a leading contributor to a global sales organization for a BPO leader, but my journey has also seen me at the helm of entire companies. Through these experiences, one truth has become undeniable: the alignment between the CEO, board, and sales strategy is absolutely critical.

Sales is the frontline, the coalface where the action unfolds. You might have the best product on the market, the most cutting-edge service, or be considered best-in-class—but if you're not selling, none of that matters. Revenue is the lifeblood of a business, and without it, even the most innovative companies can fade into obscurity.

There's something distinct about B2B sales that sets it apart from business-to-consumer (B2C) sales. In B2C, branding and emotional connection reign supreme. Why does one consumer choose Coke over Pepsi when the products are nearly identical?

In B2B, the relationship is more complex. Trust, accountability, and credibility take center stage. It's not just about what you're selling; it's about the relationship you build with your potential buyers. You want to become a trusted advisor so that when the time comes to make a decision, the first person they turn to is you. No hard selling, no cold calls—just genuine help when they need it.

Earlier in my career, I took the traditional route that most sales professionals follow: countless calls, lunches, and endless networking at events. That's how you get noticed.

However, about a decade ago, I began experimenting with social sales strategies. It started with a simple blog where I shared insights and ideas I was hearing from clients —nothing promotional, just honest thoughts on customer experience and company culture. You can find my first blog linked at the end of this foreword.

What I discovered was powerful.

By engaging my network with authentic content about the topics that mattered to them, I wasn't just starting conversations — I was building relationships. Over the years, this approach has led to real, measurable business success. Not in terms of likes or page views, but in the number of meaningful conversations with clients and prospects that have resulted in new opportunities.

Social sales won't fill your pipeline overnight. But it can build credibility, foster relationships, and create opportunities with people who would never respond to a cold email or direct sales pitch. Most B2B buyers don't want to be sold to—but when they have a problem, they do want to turn to someone they trust.

Mark's book distills this entire process beautifully. It's both a detailed guide and a simple, actionable plan: just start. Post a few blogs or share your thoughts regularly, and in a year's time, you'll have built a significant foundation of content that reflects your expertise.

Social sales isn't about feel-good posts on LinkedIn. It's about proving your authority in your industry, demonstrating your trustworthiness, and showing that you have valuable ideas for the future of your field.

To echo a question Mark poses in Chapter One: when a prospect searches for you on LinkedIn or Google, what will they find?

Will they see nothing? Outdated content from years ago? Or will they discover a leading authority who regularly shares insights that could be pivotal to their business?

That's the person they'll want to meet for coffee.

Paul O Hara
Tyneside, United Kingdom
September 24, 2024

bit.ly/paulohara
bit.ly/paulfirstblog

Preface and Introduction

Before I start, the introduction itself needs an introduction. I'm not a salesperson and I never have been, unless you can count my experience walking door-to-door offering to wash cars 'for whatever amount you think is reasonable' when I was a teenager. On a side-note, my work with the British Department for Education resulted from details like this being on my LinkedIn profile - Mark once stacked apples in a Safeway supermarket…

So why are you reading a book about B2B sales written by someone who hasn't ever worked professionally in sales?

The connection is that I have spent many years directly supporting salespeople and sales teams. I've worked closely with everyone from junior sales team members - with no public profile - to sales directors and CEOs with an international reputation.

My experience working with people at many different levels within many different companies, and in many countries, has given me some valuable insight into how content can support the sales process.

I've never been paid a bonus for success - I'm just paid for the work I deliver - but sometimes when I have heard about a big contract win that is worth millions of dollars I have smiled and thought that maybe the writer should have been paid 1% of that as a bonus!

It's happened more than once, which led me to think that I really should collect together some ideas on what really works all in one place.

My own experience seems fairly unique as I have come from a background in coding, technology, and the management of tech projects and switched career into writing. Most people I meet in this field have studied and worked in marketing, but it usually works well for me to say that I used to be a technology director when I'm proposing to a technology director that I could be their ghost.

So let's turn to the real introduction. How did I get started in this area and why should you continue reading this book?

I stumbled into the world of social sales. It was never my intention to make a living as a ghost writer, but it suited my skills and it's a more flexible life than the endless meetings people suffer in most corporate environments.

Let's go back to the beginning. I studied computer science and software engineering and my first few jobs were in coding. I eventually found myself on a bank trading floor designing software that could help the traders identify gaps in the market - we even called one of my arbitrage applications 'Bonanza…'

Eventually I was a systems analyst, designing bespoke bank software without coding it - I designed it and the coders did their thing. There was a presentation by the senior management about a new business the bank planned to launch. The CIO said we are going to launch this as soon as we have a technology system ready to support the business team.

I had just been to the office in Singapore, working on some equity trading software we had built internally. The CIO needed an equity trading system. With some confidence I waved from the audience and said, we have a system in Asia that can do 80-90% of what you need. We just need to customize it.

The CIO called me over at the end of the meeting. Within minutes I was no longer an analyst, I had my own project and budget and I could do whatever was needed to get this new business off the ground.

Eventually I headed all the equity trading technology in this bank and during my tenure as a technology director we moved a significant amount of work over to Bengaluru in India - then known as Bangalore.

I started exploring various books about India. I read about the history and culture as well as some of the tourism guides, but I couldn't find any contemporary exploration of what was happening to the technology industry in India.

So I wrote about it and my first book was published in 2004 by Springer in Germany. It was well reviewed and I decided to leave the day to day office environment and focus my attention on writing about technology. Seeing praise about your own book in The Financial Times can make people think that writing is a viable career option.

I was never really a professional journalist, but I managed to get some of my commentary in interesting places, including The Financial Times, the BBC, and The Observer. However, I also found that relying on book sales and sporadic journalism is entirely different to getting a monthly salary from a large company.

I had started blogging regularly for Computing and then Computer Weekly during the early 2000s - both national technology trade journals in the UK. These blogs were an integral part of both magazines and allowed me the immediacy to write an article on any subject any time I wanted - the editor would pick a blog to use in the print magazine.

I was noticed by a major Indian technology company. They asked if I could start ghostwriting ideas about the future of technology that would be published by the head of their consulting group.

This sounded great - I just write some opinion and get paid to allow someone else to publish it.

Then I was being contacted by some politicians in both the UK and India, asking me to help them with speeches. I think they were probably tipped off by the Indian High Commissioner (ambassador) in London, who I had helped quite often with speeches or advice on existing speeches that needed him to comment on technology.

An international telco contacted me and asked if I could spend time ghosting speeches, presentations, and articles for their CEO.

I hadn't planned this at all. I had left the corporate world convinced that some good reviews and a few books with my name on them would be enough to carve out a new career. I soon found that only a tiny percentage of writers live primarily from their royalties - the books are usually a way for them to get other work.

However this soon developed into the type of portfolio career that Charles Handy had been writing about since the 1980s. Do some media work. Work on a new book. Focus on some corporate writing. Then keep Friday free for admin and invoices. Soon, I had more than a dozen clients asking me to ghost for them.

In the early days this was type of work was considered to be marketing. I even wrote a book about 'content marketing' back in 2015, which explored some of my experience writing blogs for executives at that time. Although that book has dated, some of the ideas are still very relevant.

I gradually noticed a change in how clients were asking me to write. Instead of just saying, we want to be seen as the best in a specific area so go ahead and write about that subject - make us look interesting and forward-thinking - there were more specific requests to be noticed.

For example, I'd get a request from a company that sells services to retailers saying 'talk about this technology, but make sure you talk about some of the issues faced by RETAILER X.'

Or someone would say, this new report by Forrester Research is good, but they forgot some important points. Why don't we comment on that and it will also get us noticed by the analysts there?

Or this article in the New York Times talks about our industry, but doesn't mention half of what is really important. Let's comment on it and use LinkedIn to make sure the journalist notices what we are saying.

The content was no longer just being used to build credibility as someone who knows their industry. It was being weaponized and targeted at the people that could affect the fortunes of that business.

- Who are our prospective clients? Let's write about those companies, using them as examples of companies that might need to consider reviewing their technology choices.

- Which industry analysts do our clients listen to? We need to get in front of those analysts and impress them with our vision of the future.

- Which news journals are our prospective clients reading? When major business journalists are talking about our industry are they calling us for comment or interviews?

- Can we massage the ego of existing clients by publishing articles that mention them as a good example of a company that understands how their industry works today?

A couple of my clients embraced this change and we experienced some major success together. I saw executives winning awards for their content, being invited to deliver keynote speeches at conferences because of their blogs, and winning contracts because we had alerted executives to some ideas by blogging about them.. which led to a coffee and discussion and eventually a contract.

I talked to some more of my clients and eventually the whole idea of content marketing morphed into social sales. This was now entirely about supporting sales directors and c-level executives - helping them to not just project an image of credibility, but helping them to get noticed.

Then Covid happened and my workload tripled almost overnight. The pandemic visibly proved that people could work more flexibly in terms of both work location and work hours. It also proved that you can make connections and get noticed using content and social networks. Social sales was real.

One of my my clients said to me, we will take as much from you as you can possibly write. How could I say no? After all, all of my travel had been cancelled. The holiday I had planned with my wife to go and see Elvis Presley's home in Memphis never happened - although I did actually get a refund for those tickets.

People can now fly to meetings and conferences once again, but the lessons many sales executives learned during the pandemic are still highly relevant. You can build credibility and trust through the use of content and this is essential for B2B sales.

This short book is an exploration of how and why social sales works, based on my own experience of professional writing about technology and businesses using technology going back over two decades.

I'm sure you can find many other stories from people on the frontline of sales, but this is the story of a writer who has supported salespeople all over the world for the past two decades. I hope you enjoy it.

Mark Hillary
São Paulo, Brazil
September 27, 2024
markhillary.com

CHAPTER ONE

Covid Changed Everything

The Key Takeaways

The Covid-19 pandemic drastically shifted how B2B sales executives approached building trust and credibility, as in-person meetings and traditional networking events became impossible. As businesses quickly adapted to remote work, sales teams were forced to rely on digital platforms and online content to engage with prospects and clients.

Instead of face-to-face interactions, they turned to virtual communication and content-driven strategies, leveraging blogs, webinars, case studies, and social media to showcase expertise and nurture relationships. This pivot emphasized the importance of digital presence, requiring sales executives to create consistent, high-quality content to maintain visibility and build trust, all while adapting to a rapidly changing and more competitive online marketplace.

The use of social media to build the profile of a business and individual sales executives has been a growing trend for many years. I have been helping companies to publish information on blogs since before social media was even available, but it was really the 2010s when this become an important communication strategy for sales executives.

In 2016 the Harvard Business Review published research by Laurence Minsky of Columbia College Chicago, and Keith A. Queensberry of Messiah College in Mechanicsburg, PA.[1] This detailed just how much business to business (B2B) sales had changed in the era of social media.

Some of the most important statistics or points raised in this HBR research include:

- It now takes at least 18 phone calls to connect to a prospect
- Callback rates from prospects are less than 1%
- Only 24% of outbound sales emails are ever opened
- 84% of B2B buyers start out from a referral not contact from a salesperson
- Peer recommendations now influence over 90% of all B2B buying decisions
- 82% of B2B buyers said that the social content of their chosen supplier had a significant impact on their buying decision
- 72% of B2B salespeople who use social media actively as a part of their job report that they outperform their peers.

As the HBR article says: "Social sales content also gets salespeople involved earlier in the sales cycle, which means they're more likely to define the criteria for an ideal solution or the "buying vision," and thus, more likely to win the sale."2

The problem was clear even back in 2016. Sales teams value and prioritize making sales, not fixing the problems faced by their potential client. They just want to make that sale and the B2B buyers know it, so they do all they can to avoid salespeople.

Self-service sales is also an increasing reality for many B2B services. The Dow Chemical Company is one of the largest producers of chemicals in the world - they sell to businesses, not individual customers. However, as Daniel Hay, the CX and Digital Transformation Leader (Latam), at Dow explained to me on my own CX Files podcast in 2022, this major B2B company looked at Amazon and drew inspiration from a traditional online retail site.3

Dow found that if they made it easier to select the products that a B2B buyer needs, then the buyer could easily select and purchase what they need, set up repeat or recurring orders, and manage the account without an interaction from a sales executive.

Make B2B sales as easy to use as Amazon and the buyer can do it all online - self-service comes to the B2B environment.

Social sales, or social selling, is distinct from social marketing. When brands use social media to promote a product or just to generate brand awareness, they are not directly selling.

What we will focus on in this book is how sales teams can use the social tools everyone is now familiar with to be more successful.

But let's start out by considering one of those statistics from the HBR study back in 2016: 82% of B2B buyers said that the social content of their chosen supplier had a significant impact on their buying decision.

Now consider what happened in 2020 and through into 2021. The Covid-19 pandemic created a situation where most countries around the world placed restrictions on meetings, events, and travel. I didn't travel at all for both of those two years, even though the restrictions had eased throughout 2021.

B2B sales executives could not meet prospects or existing clients. They could not attend any conferences or sales events. They could not network with industry contacts over drinks or dinner. All their usual tactics were impossible.

The only way to stay visible during that time was to publish opinion, ideas, and thought leadership. Sales executives had to show that they were full of ideas and still relevant, without any of the usual social interactions that help them to reinforce this.

LinkedIn was suddenly flooded with corporate webinars and online events to the extent that many of us still feel scarred by the experience of sitting through one terrible webinar after another.

However, the smart executives used this time to build a profile. They published ideas that went far beyond just promoting their products, they showed how deep they understand their business and industry and hinted at the knowledge they could share if they were hired to help a company.

Covid changed everything. If 82% of B2B buyers were influenced by your online content in 2016 then just think how many are now influenced by what you post online today? It must now be almost every single B2B buyer - almost 100%.

So what happens when a prospective buyer searches Google or LinkedIn for the name of your sales director or CEO? Do they find a wealth of informed opinion and ideas or just a PowerPoint from ten years ago?

I knew this was becoming important when I heard from the CEO of a tech company in Ireland. He and I had been on a late night out in London in 2008 - he ended up on stage in a bar singing Elvis songs that I had recorded on my phone and uploaded to YouTube.

Many years after this happened, he sent a frantic text message begging me to delete the video - or at least remove his name - because every time his company was bidding for contracts he would be reminded by the potential client "oh, we love that Elvis video!"

It was fun, but not really the right image to send when bidding for government contracts all over the world.

That was about the middle of the 2010s. Prospective customers were already Googling the name of the CEO before a meeting back then. What are they finding online when they search for what your own CEO or sales director has been up to?

So let's take a step back and introduce the book. It is clear that social sales was important before the pandemic, but a social profile for sales teams and individual sales leaders is now critical in the post-pandemic business environment.

How can we summarize the growth of social sales in the past 10-15 years and set the scene for what has happened and what needs to be done?

Let's try building a blueprint for what your business needs to do.

The use of social sales for B2B companies has grown significantly throughout the 2010s, driven by the increasing prevalence of social media as a tool for building trust, relationships, and credibility in the business world.

Here's an overview of how social sales evolved during that period:

1. **Shift from Traditional Sales to Digital Sales**
    - **Early 2010s:** At the start of the decade, B2B sales were still largely reliant on traditional methods such as cold calling, email marketing, and face-to-face meetings. However, as social media platforms like LinkedIn, Twitter/X, and later Instagram and TikTok began to grow in popularity, salespeople started using these channels to connect with prospects in a more personalized, non-intrusive way.
    - **Late 2010s:** By the end of the decade, social selling had become a key component of B2B sales strategies. Social media allowed sales professionals to research prospects, engage with decision-makers, and position themselves as trusted advisors by sharing relevant content.

2. **Building Trust and Credibility**
   - **Content Sharing and Thought Leadership:** B2B companies began to realize that social media could be used not just for brand awareness but also to build trust by sharing insightful content, thought leadership articles, case studies, and industry news. Sales teams increasingly used platforms like LinkedIn to share valuable information with their networks, positioning their companies as credible experts in their fields.
   - **Engagement and Personalization:** Unlike traditional cold outreach, social selling allowed for more personalized engagement with prospects. B2B sales professionals used social media to comment on industry discussions, join LinkedIn groups, and engage with content shared by potential clients. This approach helped build trust by establishing relationships in a more natural, conversational way.

3. **Data-Driven Sales Strategies**
   - **Social Listening and Insights:** As social platforms evolved, they offered more tools for sales professionals to track and analyze the behavior of potential customers. Sales teams could monitor social media interactions, track engagement, and gather insights into customer pain points and industry trends. This allowed B2B companies to craft more targeted sales approaches.
   - **Lead Generation:** Social media platforms introduced sophisticated advertising and

analytics tools that enabled B2B companies to run targeted campaigns. Sales teams could identify and nurture leads more effectively, using data-driven strategies to focus on high-value prospects who were actively engaging with their content or showing interest in similar products and services.

4. **Rise of LinkedIn as a Sales Powerhouse**
   - **LinkedIn's Dominance:** Throughout the 2010s, LinkedIn became the leading platform for B2B social selling. It transformed from a job-seeking and professional networking platform into a sales powerhouse where companies could showcase their expertise, connect with decision-makers, and build a professional brand. LinkedIn Sales Navigator, launched in 2014, provided advanced tools for finding leads, managing accounts, and engaging with prospects, further enhancing its appeal for B2B sales professionals.[4]
   - **Employee Advocacy:** B2B companies began encouraging their employees, particularly sales teams, to become brand advocates on social media. By sharing company updates, industry insights, and thought leadership content, employees helped extend the company's reach, build credibility, and generate leads.

5. **Trust and Relationship Building in the Digital Age**
   - **Humanizing the Sales Process:** Social selling helped humanize the B2B sales process by allowing salespeople to engage with prospects on

a personal level before making any sales pitches. Through social media, they could showcase their expertise, offer advice, and demonstrate genuine interest in solving customer problems, which built trust and long-term relationships.

- **Reviews and Recommendations:** Platforms like LinkedIn allowed clients and partners to leave recommendations and endorsements for B2B companies and their salespeople. Positive testimonials and peer recommendations became powerful tools for building trust and attracting new prospects.

6. **The Role of Content in Social Selling**
    - **Educating Buyers:** By the mid-2010s, the B2B buying process had changed. Buyers were conducting much of their research online before ever speaking to a salesperson. Social media became a critical channel for B2B companies to share educational content that helped prospects understand their needs, explore solutions, and make informed purchasing decisions.
    - **Video and Visual Content:** Toward the end of the decade, visual content like videos, infographics, and webinars became key tools for B2B social selling. Video content, in particular, helped companies explain complex products and services more effectively while building trust and credibility with audiences. Look at a sales executive such as Stephanie Reeves Millner for an example of someone who regularly uses short videos to update followers on thoughts and ideas.[5]

7. **Fostering Long-Term Relationships and Customer Retention**

- **Post-Sale Engagement:** Social selling didn't stop at acquiring new customers. B2B companies used social media to maintain relationships with existing clients, offering them continued value through updates, support, and industry insights. This approach helped foster long-term customer loyalty and turned clients into advocates for the brand.

- **Community Building:** Some companies even created online communities around their brand or product, offering spaces for customers, partners, and prospects to interact, share ideas, and provide feedback. This further strengthened trust and engagement.

The 2010s saw the transformation of social media from a peripheral tool to a central component of B2B sales strategies. Social sales helped B2B companies build trust and credibility by fostering genuine relationships with prospects and customers.

By using platforms like LinkedIn to engage with decision-makers, share thought leadership, and leverage data-driven insights, sales professionals were able to build a more personalized and consultative sales approach, ultimately driving growth and long-term success.

Social selling continues to evolve and is now an integral part of how B2B companies connect with their target audiences.

References:

1. https://hbr.org/2016/11/84-of-b2b-sales-start-with-a-referral-not-a-salesperson
2. https://www.saleswingsapp.com/how-to/leverage-sales-trigger-events/
3. https://cxfiles.libsyn.com/cxfiles/daniel-hay-dow-designing-a-fantastic-b2b-customer-experience
4. https://www.linkedin.com/business/sales/blog/sales-navigator/introducing-a-brief-history-of-linkedin-sales-navigator-infogra
5. https://www.linkedin.com/in/stephaniemillner/recent-activity/all/

CHAPTER TWO

Why Is Social Sales So Important Today?

The Key Takeaways

Social sales has become essential for B2B sales executives because modern buyers increasingly rely on digital channels to research solutions and make purchasing decisions. Social platforms like LinkedIn provide a direct way for sales professionals to engage with prospects, showcase expertise, and build relationships long before formal sales discussions take place.

As traditional methods like cold calling become less effective, social selling enables sales teams to reach potential clients where they are active, fostering trust and credibility through meaningful interactions. By integrating social media into their strategy, B2B sales executives can better understand their audience, offer relevant content, and ultimately drive more personalized and effective sales engagements.

In the digital age, the landscape of B2B (business-to-business) sales has undergone a transformative shift. Traditional sales techniques, while still relevant, are increasingly supplemented—and in some cases, replaced—by digital strategies that leverage the power of social media.

Millennials are in their 40s and early Generation Z adults are now fast approaching 30 so there are millions of B2B sales professionals that were introduced to smartphones and digital communication when they were still children.[1]

Among the many different social platforms available, LinkedIn stands out as a particularly potent tool for B2B salespeople. As the world's largest professional networking site, LinkedIn is where business relationships are formed, industry insights are shared, and, crucially, sales opportunities are generated. In tandem with the pervasive influence of Google as the primary search engine, these platforms have become indispensable for sales teams aiming to maintain visibility and credibility in an increasingly competitive market.

This chapter explores why LinkedIn and Google visibility is now so essential for B2B salespeople, delving into the changing dynamics of buyer behavior, the benefits of digital engagement, and the strategic advantages of a strong online presence.

The Evolution of B2B Sales and Buyer Behavior

To understand the growing importance of LinkedIn and Google for B2B sales, it is essential to first consider the evolution of buyer behavior in the digital age. Today's B2B buyers are more informed and self-sufficient than ever before. A significant shift has occurred where buyers now conduct extensive research online before engaging with a sales representative.

According to a study by Gartner, up to 57% of the purchase decision process is completed before a buyer ever reaches out to a supplier or vendor.[2] This means that by the time a sales representative is contacted, the buyer has already formed a strong opinion about the product, the company, and even the salesperson.

This shift in behavior underscores the critical need for salespeople to be visible during the early stages of the buyer's journey. If potential clients cannot find a salesperson or their company during their research phase, they are likely to turn to competitors who are more visible and active online.

LinkedIn, as a professional network, is a key platform where these initial research activities often take place. Salespeople who maintain a strong presence on LinkedIn can engage with potential clients long before a formal sales process begins, influencing their perceptions and positioning themselves as trusted advisors rather than just vendors pitching for sales.

Building Credibility and Trust Through LinkedIn

One of the primary reasons LinkedIn has become so crucial for B2B sales is its ability to build and convey credibility. In B2B transactions, trust is paramount. Buyers need to feel confident not only in the product or service being offered but also in the people behind it.

LinkedIn allows salespeople to showcase their expertise, share relevant content, and engage in industry-specific discussions, all of which contribute to building a reputation as a knowledgeable and trustworthy professional.

In the 2020s career guidance experts now call it a 'red flag' if you don't have a LinkedIn profile. It's seen as evasive, there is something about your career that is hidden.[3]

LinkedIn profiles used to serve as little more than digital resumes, but they now go beyond that by providing a platform for salespeople to highlight their achievements, endorsements, and recommendations from colleagues and clients.

These elements create a narrative around the salesperson's professional capabilities and successes, offering proof points that can be compelling for potential clients. In addition, by sharing insightful content—whether through posts, articles, or engagement with others' content—salespeople can demonstrate their deep understanding of industry trends and challenges.

This positions them as thought leaders, which is particularly important in complex B2B sales where the decision-making process is often lengthy and involves multiple stakeholders.

The Role of LinkedIn in Relationship Building

B2B sales are inherently relational. The success of a sale often hinges on the relationship between the salesperson and the client. LinkedIn facilitates relationship building in a way that traditional sales methods cannot. By connecting with prospects, clients, and industry peers, salespeople can expand their professional networks, stay updated on key industry developments, and maintain ongoing communication with their connections - it helps to build a rapport.[4]

LinkedIn's messaging and connection features allow salespeople to engage with prospects in a non-intrusive manner. Instead of cold calling or emailing, which can be perceived as pushy, LinkedIn offers a more natural way to initiate conversations.

Salespeople can comment on a prospect's post, share relevant articles, or simply engage in a discussion thread, all of which can lead to more meaningful interactions. This method of engagement is less about selling and more about providing value, which can help to build stronger, more authentic relationships over time.

Additionally, LinkedIn allows salespeople to stay top-of-mind with their network. Regular updates, whether through posts or shared content, keep the salesperson visible to their connections. This ongoing visibility is crucial because it ensures that when a prospect is ready to make a purchase decision, the salesperson is already in their consideration set.

The Strategic Advantage of Google Visibility

While LinkedIn is a powerful platform for building professional relationships and credibility, Google remains the primary tool for research and information gathering. When potential clients search for information about a company or a specific individual, Google is often their first stop. This makes it essential for B2B salespeople to manage their online presence beyond LinkedIn, ensuring that their professional profile and content are easily discoverable on Google.

Search itself is in the process of changing at the time this book was written. Artificial Intelligence is being used in search tools such as Google, Perplexity, and Bing to suggest complete answers to search questions, rather than just offering a link to a page, however the basic point remains the same - what does a potential client find when they search for information about you online?[5]

Google visibility can be enhanced through various means, including SEO (search engine optimization), content marketing, and online reviews. For salespeople, it is important to ensure that their LinkedIn profiles are optimized for search engines. This includes using relevant keywords in their profile descriptions, job titles, and content. Additionally, participating in industry blogs, contributing to online publications, and being featured in media can all help to boost a salesperson's Google search ranking.

Cross-posting content that is primarily designed for LinkedIn to an industry journal or blog can be a useful way to enhance general search results - especially when the person searching is specifically scanning news sources. A salesperson involved in customer service should always post their articles and content on a site like Customer Think because this will feature in Google News searches.⁶

The strategic advantage of being easily found on Google cannot be overstated. In a competitive B2B environment, being the first name that appears in a prospect's search results can make a significant difference. It not only increases the likelihood of initial contact but also helps in establishing credibility right from the start.

A well-managed online presence on Google, combined with an active LinkedIn profile, creates a comprehensive digital footprint that enhances a salesperson's visibility and appeal.

Leveraging Social Proof and Endorsements

Another critical aspect of using social media like LinkedIn for B2B sales is the concept of social proof. Social proof refers to the psychological phenomenon where people are influenced by the actions and opinions of others. On LinkedIn, social proof can take the form of endorsements, recommendations, and the visible connections a salesperson has within the industry.

Endorsements for specific skills help to validate a salesperson's expertise in key areas relevant to potential clients. Recommendations from colleagues, superiors, and especially clients, add a layer of authenticity to the salesperson's profile, making them more attractive to prospects. When a potential client sees that others in the industry have endorsed and recommended a salesperson, it builds trust and reduces perceived risk.

This does not even need to be in the formal endorsements or recommendations section of a LinkedIn profile - even ongoing conversations on posts will demonstrate what others think of the information this person is posting.

LinkedIn's network visibility allows potential clients to see mutual connections, which can be a powerful form of social proof. If a prospect sees that they share connections with a salesperson, they may be more inclined to trust that salesperson based on the credibility of their shared contacts.

This interconnectedness is a unique feature of LinkedIn that enhances the traditional referral process, making it easier for salespeople to leverage their existing network to generate new leads.

The Imperative of Digital Presence in B2B Sales

The importance of using social media platforms like LinkedIn, in conjunction with maintaining a strong presence on Google, has become a critical component of B2B sales strategy. The evolution of buyer behavior, the necessity of building credibility and trust, the importance of relationship building, and the strategic advantages of visibility all point to the same conclusion: a robust online presence is no longer optional—it is imperative.

You may know some old-school sales executives who still believe that the expensive dinner, or visit to a race track, cannot be beaten as a way of getting to know a potential client. Personal contact and interaction will always remain important, but it is much more likely in this era of sales that a visit to the hospitality area at a big game started out as a LinkedIn interaction.

In 2022, the Harvard Business Review even went so far as to call traditional B2B sales practices 'obsolete' - the future is quite obviously digital.[7]

For B2B salespeople, being visible on LinkedIn and Google means being present where their potential clients are searching, researching, and forming opinions. It is about engaging with prospects early in their buying journey, establishing themselves as thought leaders, and building relationships that are grounded in trust and mutual value.

As the digital landscape continues to evolve, those who embrace these platforms and use them effectively will be best positioned to succeed in the increasingly competitive world of B2B sales.

References:

1. https://en.wikipedia.org/wiki/Generation_Z
2. https://www.gartner.com/smarterwithgartner/power-challenger-sales-model
3. https://www.cnbc.com/2023/09/11/linkedin-red-flags.html
4. https://blog.hootsuite.com/what-is-social-selling/
5. https://www.zdnet.com/article/best-ai-search-engine/
6. https://customerthink.com/
7. https://hbr.org/2022/02/traditional-b2b-sales-and-marketing-are-becoming-obsolete

CHAPTER THREE

Target Audience Identification

The Key Takeaways

A B2B social sales strategy can identify the target audience for content by first defining the ideal customer profile (ICP) based on factors like industry, company size, job role, and specific business challenges. By analyzing current clients and using tools like LinkedIn's advanced search, sales executives can pinpoint key decision-makers and influencers who align with their ICP.

Social listening tools also play a role, allowing sales teams to monitor discussions, trends, and keywords relevant to their industry, helping them refine their audience targeting. This combination of research, social listening, and data analysis ensures that content is tailored to the right audience, addressing their needs and pain points.

Who is your ideal customer?

Building a social sales strategy for B2B companies requires a deep understanding of the ideal customer profile (ICP) and identifying the key industry influencers and decision-makers who can amplify your message.

For a sales executive, these steps involve research, targeting, and content strategy, ensuring that social content reaches the right people and drives engagement.[1]

Here's a few ideas on how to define an ICP and identify key influencers and decision-makers:

1. Defining the Ideal Customer Profile (ICP) for Social Content

An Ideal Customer Profile (ICP) is a description of the type of company that would gain the most value from your product or service. Defining an ICP allows sales executives to create content that resonates with the right audience.

The process typically includes these steps:

- **A. Analyze Current Best Customers**
  - Identify Patterns: Look at your existing customer base, especially your top-performing clients. What are the common traits among them? Analyze demographic (or firmographic in the case of a business), and behavioral data, such as:

- **Company Size:** How large is the company in terms of revenue, employee count, or market presence?
- **Industry:** What industries are most aligned with your offering?
- **Geography:** Where are your best customers located?
- **Pain Points:** What common problems do your current customers face that your product solves?

- **Outcome:** Use these insights to create a detailed profile that includes the types of companies, the decision-makers you typically deal with, and their key challenges.

B. Define Buyer Personas

- Identify Decision-Makers: Within your ICP, define the key buyer personas—individuals who have decision-making power or influence in the purchasing process. This might include roles such as:
    - CEOs for small businesses
    - CIOs, CTOs, or IT Managers for tech-related solutions
    - Procurement Officers for large enterprises
    - Marketing Directors for solutions related to customer outreach or branding
- **Tailor Content to Personas:** Develop content that speaks directly to the concerns and needs of each persona. For example, a CTO might

be interested in technical efficiency, while a CEO may focus on cost savings or strategic alignment.

C. Understand Buyer Behavior

- **Social Media Presence:** Research where your target customers spend their time online. Are they active on LinkedIn, Twitter/X, or industry-specific forums? Focus on creating content tailored to the platforms they frequent.
- **Content Preferences:** Understand the types of content your ICP consumes—whether it's thought leadership articles, case studies, webinars, or short social media posts. The more closely your content aligns with their preferences, the better.

D. Monitor Competitors' Audiences

- **Analyze Competitors:** Observe the audience your competitors are engaging with on social platforms. This can provide insights into which types of companies and decision-makers are already interested in similar solutions, allowing you to refine your ICP and create more targeted content.

2. Identifying Key Industry Influencers and Decision-Makers

Once the ICP is defined, the next step is to identify the influencers and decision-makers who can amplify your social content and help drive engagement. These individuals can help build credibility, expand your reach, and bring you closer to key decision-makers in the target companies.

Traditionally, B2B influencers would have been industry analysts or business journalists, but this is no longer strictly true. Those with reach and influence may have no formal connection to a business journal or analyst firm today.

A. Leverage LinkedIn for Influencer and Decision-Maker Research

- **Advanced Search Filters:** LinkedIn offers advanced search filters (especially with LinkedIn Sales Navigator) that allow you to identify key decision-makers based on industry, job title, seniority, and company size.

- **Group Participation:** Join LinkedIn groups relevant to your industry and pay attention to the most active contributors. These individuals are often influencers or well-connected professionals whose opinions shape industry conversations.

- **Follow and Engage:** Follow and engage with influencers and decision-makers by liking, sharing, and commenting on their posts. Building rapport over time will increase the likelihood that they'll engage with your content in return.

B. Use Industry-Specific Tools and Platforms

- **Social Listening Tools:** Tools like Hootsuite, BuzzSumo, or Brandwatch can help identify the most influential voices in your industry. These tools track mentions, hashtags, and trends, allowing you to discover who is leading conversations that align with your business.

- **Twitter/X Lists:** Create Twitter/X lists to follow key industry influencers. Monitoring these lists will help you stay updated on their content and engage with them in real time. Although the value of X has significantly declined as a platform where business executives interact, it is still packed full of journalists and influencers.[2]

C. **Monitor Industry Events and Publications**
- **Conference Speakers:** Pay attention to speakers and thought leaders at industry conferences and webinars. These individuals are often well-respected in their fields and have large followings on social media.
- **Trade Publications and Blogs:** Identify contributors to leading industry publications, as they often hold influential positions in their companies and industries. These contributors may also share their insights on social media platforms, providing opportunities for engagement.
- **Podcasts:** Listen to industry podcasts where key decision-makers or influencers are interviewed. These platforms often provide insights into thought leaders who have strong followings and whose endorsements can amplify your social reach. CX Files is a good example.[3]

D. **Use Employee Advocacy Programs**
- **Encourage Internal Networking:** Empower your sales team and other employees to use their personal LinkedIn profiles to engage with decision-makers and influencers. Employee

advocacy programs can extend your brand's reach by allowing your team to share content with their networks - this can be a powerful way for sales teams to amplify their own content - by coordinating a sales team so you all share each others content.

- **Content Creation and Sharing:** Encourage your employees to share thought leadership content, case studies, and insights that are relevant to the target audience. Decision-makers are more likely to engage with content that comes from trusted, authentic voices.[4]

Often this just requires some basic organization within a sales team so that when one team member posts a new piece of content on LinkedIn, they always alert the rest of the team and the team always shares to their own network. It's simple, but has a very strong amplification effect.

3. Content Strategy to Appeal to ICP and Influencers

To ensure your social content captures the attention of your ICP and key influencers, the strategy must focus on relevance, value, and engagement.

Here's how to align content with your audience's needs:

A. Create Valuable, Insightful Content

- **Address Pain Points:** Focus on creating content that solves the specific problems of your ICP. This could include case studies, white papers, webinars, and blog posts that showcase how your product or service delivers results.

- **Thought Leadership:** Position your company as a leader in the industry by sharing research reports, expert opinions, and industry trends. Influencers and decision-makers are more likely to share and engage with content that offers value and new perspectives.

B. **Use Data-Driven Content**
- **Infographics and Reports:** B2B decision-makers often rely on data when making purchasing decisions. Infographics, charts, and detailed reports backed by industry statistics are highly shareable and can capture the attention of both decision-makers and influencers.

C. **Engage in Social Conversations**
- **Join Industry Discussions:** Participate in conversations on social media platforms where decision-makers and influencers are already active. By offering thoughtful insights and adding value to these conversations, you can gradually build relationships and increase your visibility.
- **Use Hashtags and Keywords:** Incorporate relevant hashtags and keywords to make your content discoverable. This is particularly useful on Twitter/X, LinkedIn, and Instagram, where industry hashtags can help your content reach a wider audience.

D. **Encourage Influencer Partnerships**
- **Collaborate with Industry Experts:** Consider co-creating content with influencers or thought leaders in your industry. This could include joint

webinars, interviews, or blog contributions that benefit both parties and increase your visibility among the influencer's audience.

- **Tag Influencers:** When sharing content on social media, tag relevant influencers or decision-makers who might find the content valuable. This can encourage them to engage with or share your post, expanding your reach.

By clearly defining the ideal customer profile, identifying key industry influencers and decision-makers, and crafting targeted, valuable content, sales executives can build a strong social sales strategy. Leveraging platforms like LinkedIn and Twitter/X to engage with these key figures not only enhances visibility but also fosters trust, driving long-term business relationships.

A simple rule to think about is to always ensure that your content is focused on ideas, predictions, or pain points and solutions. This ensures that it can offer value to a potential reader. If your content is little more than 'here is what our company does and let me talk all about it…' then it is unlikely to be seen as useful.

Would it be interesting enough for someone to share to their network? This is the most basic rule of thumb. Is your thought leadership comparable to an article in Forbes or The Economist - something a B2B buyer would share to their network with a comment saying 'this is interesting…'? Or does it just say 'buy our stuff…'?

It is also worth noting that some channels - such as a podcast - may not develop a large audience, but the platform can be used for influencer collaboration and contacting prospects. Your podcast may be focused on a niche area, but so long as the right people hear about it then it is performing a sales function.[5]

References:

1. https://www.melottimedia.com.au/blog/how-to-define-your-ideal-customers-in-10-steps-html/
2. https://www.theglobeandmail.com/business/commentary/article-twitter-was-once-a-valuable-business-tool-x-is-now-a-mess/
3. https://cxfiles.libsyn.com/cxfiles
4. https://www.forbes.com/councils/forbesbusinesscouncil/2023/05/09/how-to-empower-employees-to-build-their-personal-brand-on-social/
5. https://improvepodcast.com/how-many-listeners-you-need

CHAPTER FOUR

Building Your Content Strategy

The Key Takeaways

Building a robust content strategy is crucial for a B2B social sales strategy because it allows sales executives to consistently deliver value to prospects and clients through relevant, insightful, and engaging content. High-quality content helps address the specific pain points and needs of the target audience, positioning the sales team as trusted experts and thought leaders.

By offering solutions and educating potential buyers, rather than pushing a direct sale, the content fosters trust and long-term relationships. A well-planned content strategy ensures that the right message reaches the right people at the right time, helping to move prospects through the sales funnel while maintaining credibility and engagement.

The information presented in your content is critical for success. As mentioned in the previous chapter, if your articles and podcast appearances are only ever focused on saying "hey look at us, this is what we do and our prices are on the website" then you can forget about anyone paying attention.[1]

You are competing with everything else online for attention - news, social media, messages from friends and family. Your content needs to be engaging and interesting.

This process of building a robust content strategy for B2B social sales is crucial to effectively engage with your target audience, demonstrate thought leadership, and ultimately drive conversions.

A well-crafted content strategy ensures that you're creating high-quality, relevant content that speaks to the needs and pain points of your ideal customer profile (ICP) while establishing trust and positioning your brand as an industry leader.

Although in this chapter we are going to explore who to talk to and the types of content you can produce, the most important point is to make it useful for the prospective customer or influencer you want to notice what you are publishing.

Just make it useful.

1. Understanding Your Target Audience and Pain Points

Before creating content, it's essential to thoroughly understand your target audience—their pain points, needs, and the solutions they're seeking.

Here's how you can approach it:

Research Your Ideal Customer Profile (ICP)

- Identify common challenges or problems your audience faces. For example, if you're selling a software solution to manufacturing companies, their pain points might include supply chain inefficiencies or operational bottlenecks.
- Understand their goals and what success looks like for them. This could include improving efficiency, reducing costs, or driving innovation. Why would they call you?

Segment Your Audience

- Divide your audience into specific personas, such as IT managers, C-suite executives, or procurement officers, and create content that addresses the specific challenges faced by each group. For example, IT managers might want to know about technical features, while CEOs focus on ROI and strategic benefits.

2. Creating High-Quality, Relevant Content

Once you understand your audience, the next step is to create content that resonates with them. High-quality content is essential for building trust and demonstrating your expertise. Here's how to craft compelling content across various formats:

Blog Posts

Blog posts are a foundational element of content marketing that help attract prospects at different stages of the buyer's journey. They provide insights into industry trends, address common questions, and offer solutions to pain points.[2]

Best Practices:

- Write posts that are both informative and actionable, offering clear solutions to specific problems.
- Use SEO to ensure your blog posts are discoverable by the right audience. Research keywords that your target audience is likely to use.
- Make your posts shareable and concise, with actionable takeaways that readers can implement.
- Have an opinion. Even use news stories or analyst reports as a hook for your own thought leadership - so you comment on what is missing from a business news story.

SEO is important when you want to be found online, but always remember your target customer and what they need. You can sacrifice SEO to a certain extent if the content is focused on a prospective customer you are pursuing.

Also be aware that addressing specific pain points can lead to 'listicles' - such as '5 ways to cope with the Black Friday rush.' These articles can be useful, but often feel artificial so think carefully about how best to create an article that offers good advice.

Whitepapers

Whitepapers offer in-depth research and analysis, positioning your brand as an authoritative source of information. They are typically used for lead generation in exchange for contact details.

Best Practices:

- Provide valuable, data-driven insights that offer deep dives into industry challenges and how your solutions address them.
- Ensure the whitepaper is well-researched, properly cited, and offers a level of depth that can guide decision-making.
- Design the whitepaper with clear sections, charts, and visuals to make it easy to digest.

Although whitepapers are naturally much longer and more detailed than blogs or news articles, and need to offer more involved ideas on business solutions, they are now far shorter than the common length of just a few years ago. Typical white papers are now 1,200 - 2,500 words in length compared to 5-10x this amount within recent memory.[3]

People want information and they want ideas for solutions, but they want it to be more concise than ever. Few managers have time or patience so the more direct you can make it while still giving enough information to be useful, the better.

Case Studies

Case studies showcase real-world examples of how your product or service solved a specific problem for a customer. They demonstrate credibility and provide tangible proof of value.

Best Practices:

- Highlight the problem, the solution you provided, and the quantifiable results (e.g., cost savings, improved efficiency).
- Make the content customer-centric, focusing on the client's success and how it applies to other similar prospects.
- Use client quotes and testimonials to add authenticity.

The most powerful case studies featured named clients, especially where the company is well-known to your target group of potential customers. It can still be worth creating a case study without naming the company, but the value of saying "we worked for a major bank" compared to saying the name of the company is diminished.[4]

It's also useful to try naming the case study after the results, such as "How XYZ Bank reduced cost by 30% and increased customer satisfaction using our system."

Videos

Video content is engaging, easy to consume, and highly shareable. It can showcase products, share customer testimonials, or explain complex solutions in a more digestible format. There are also multiple video platforms available so it's easy to cross-post and sites like YouTube are closely tied into Google search results.

Best Practices:

- Keep videos short (2-3 minutes) and focused on a specific topic or solution.
- Use animations, demos, or interviews to make your content visually engaging.
- Promote your videos across social media platforms and embed them into blog posts, emails, and landing pages.

A good example to support sales would be a video showing a demo of how your software integrates with existing ERP systems - this would appeal to IT managers. Many videos can be created with a slightly different focus.

Naturally a software demo would need to be produced with a video team or with animation, but individual sales executives can create their own short videos - effectively like a video blog or comment - just using nothing more complex than their own smartphone. For this type of video it is the comment that matters rather than the lighting.[5]

Infographics

Infographics visually represent complex information, making it easier for your audience to understand data, processes, or trends.

Best Practices:

- Use infographics to present statistics, step-by-step processes, or comparisons in a visually appealing way.
- Keep the design clean and data-driven, ensuring the content is easily shareable on social media.

An infographic titled "The Impact of AI on Supply Chain Management: A Data-Driven Overview" could summarize key findings from a whitepaper or blog post. You could even use a visual infographic to promote a blog which in turn is promoting a longer and more detailed whitepaper.6

Podcasts

Podcasts are a bit like on-demand radio shows. Around 100 million Americans listen to podcasts each week so this is now a mainstream channel. It can be difficult to build a large audience for a podcast focused on a niche business area, but it can create a highly visible platform that you can use to interview clients, prospects, and influencers.7

Best Practices:

- It's best to avoid directly naming your podcast after your company - 'The Twenty-First Century Customer Service Podcast' is a much better name than 'Dave's Contact Center Podcast.' Give it a smart name like this and just state in the introduction 'this podcast is supported by Dave's Contact Centers.'
- You don't need much equipment or knowledge of audio, but you will need a few basic skills and

a microphone. Search for 'how do I start my own podcast' to find tips on how to get started.[8]

- o Check out some similar podcasts to what you are planning. Podcasts like David's Diaries are a great example of an executive making a podcast so they have a platform to engage with lots of people from their industry.[9]

B2B podcasts will usually fail if you are aiming for audiences like the BBC or NPR, but they cost very little to setup and manage and can provide a very useful platform that opens doors. Influencers in your industry may be happy to be interviewed on a podcast - the same people who would never even bother responding to your emails.

Don't judge a podcast by the audience size. Look at who it can give you access to.

3. Addressing Pain Points with Relevant Content

Almost every piece of content should be created with the audience's pain points in mind. This is how you will make it relevant to them, but there can also be exceptions for content that explores broader industry issues or start of year predictions and so on.

Here's how to craft content that directly addresses these issues:

Identify Common Challenges

- Conduct surveys, interviews, or social listening to understand the challenges your target audience is facing. This can also be done through analyzing

- search queries, social media comments, and competitor strategies.
- For example, if your audience is struggling with inefficiencies in their supply chain, write content that provides practical solutions, such as optimizing inventory management or integrating automation.

Offer Solutions

- For each pain point, create content that provides actionable insights or solutions. Avoid overly promotional language and focus on how you can help the audience solve their problems.
- Provide clear examples of how your product or service has helped others. For instance, a blog post on "How to Streamline Your Supply Chain with AI" could offer insights into best practices, tools, and case studies.

4. Utilizing Thought Leadership to Build Authority

A strong B2B social sales strategy doesn't just involve promoting your product or service—it also requires establishing your brand and key team members as thought leaders in the industry. Thought leadership builds credibility and trust with both prospects and influencers. Here's how:

Share Industry News and Insights

- Regularly share relevant industry news, reports, and research findings on platforms like LinkedIn and Twitter/X to keep your audience informed and engaged - add your comment to the news you share to give your own take.[10]

- Use your social platforms to comment on current events and trends in the industry. This positions you as an expert who understands the market and is actively engaged in thought leadership.
- **Example:** A LinkedIn post sharing an article on new government regulations affecting supply chains, accompanied by your own analysis of how businesses should prepare, positions you as an expert and opens the door for engagement.

Publish Original Research

- If possible, conduct and publish original research on industry trends, challenges, or opportunities. This can include surveys, reports, or market analyses, which further build your authority as a leader in the field.
- Collaborate with other thought leaders or academic institutions to add credibility to your findings.
- **Example:** A report titled "The 2024 State of AI in Manufacturing" could offer unique insights and attract the attention of decision makers seeking to stay ahead of trends.

Leverage Employee Advocacy

- Encourage your sales and leadership teams to share company content on their personal social media profiles. Employee advocacy amplifies your reach and demonstrates that your team members are knowledgeable experts in the field.

- Train your sales team on how to create engaging posts that share industry news, offer insights, and engage with prospects.

Host Webinars and Virtual Events

- Host webinars that allow you to share valuable information with your audience in real-time. Webinars are an excellent platform for discussing trends, offering solutions, and answering questions directly from prospects.
- Be aware that many people tired of webinars during the pandemic, but they are viewing again now and being more selective about which ones are worthy of attention.[11]
- After the event, share the recording on your social media channels and blog to reach a wider audience - in fact this is often the most important audience as even a poorly-attended webinar can have a significant life after the live event is over.
- **Example:** A webinar titled "How AI Is Transforming Manufacturing in 2024" could feature guest speakers from the industry, offering in-depth insights and generating leads for your sales team.

5. Distributing Content Across Platforms

Having high-quality content is only effective if it reaches the right audience. Here's how to ensure your content gets noticed:

Use LinkedIn for Professional Content

- LinkedIn is the most powerful platform for B2B social sales. Share blog posts, whitepapers, and case studies here to reach decision-makers. Utilize LinkedIn Sales Navigator to target specific leads and share relevant content directly with them.
- Post consistently and engage with followers by commenting, sharing, and participating in industry conversations.

Leverage Twitter/X for Quick Updates

- Share industry news, short insights, and links to longer content like blog posts or whitepapers on Twitter/X. Use hashtags to increase visibility among targeted groups.
- Engage with influencers by tagging them in relevant posts or sharing their content, encouraging reciprocal engagement.
- Remember that the Twitter/X network is far less likely to result in access to prospective clients, but it can still be helpful for engagement with influencers and the media.[12]

Repurpose Content for Multiple Formats

- Repurpose your blog posts into short LinkedIn articles, create snippets from whitepapers for social media posts, or turn case studies into video testimonials to increase engagement.

- Cross-post content across platforms to maximize reach, but tailor each post to the platform's audience and format.
- A blog can be posted as an article on LinkedIn, an SEO-friendly article on the corporate website, and on a trade journal - each outlet has a different function.

Building a robust content strategy for B2B social sales involves a deep understanding of your target audience's pain points, creating diverse content that provides valuable solutions, and establishing your company as a thought leader through consistent, insightful contributions to industry conversations.

By sharing high-quality, relevant content across multiple formats and platforms, you can engage decision-makers, build trust, and drive long-term business success.

Are you solving problems or offering ideas for their business or industry? If not then it will only ever be seen as sales and marketing pitches that can easily be ignored.

References:

1. https://chroniclerepublic.com/why-hard-selling-doesnt-work-on-social-media/
2. https://www.linkedin.com/pulse/b2b-blogging-best-practices-you-must-know-2023-company-expert
3. https://www.windmillstrategy.com/how-to-write-white-papers/
4. https://successkit.io/how-to-make-the-anonymous-case-study-work/
5. https://www.linkedin.com/pulse/creating-engaging-b2b-sales-videos-drive-success-b2b-rocket-wmane/
6. https://blog.quuu.co/infographics-content-marketing/
7. https://www.edisonresearch.com/podcast-listening-hits-record-highs/
8. https://www.linkedin.com/pulse/how-do-i-start-my-own-podcast-mark-hillary/
9. https://bit.ly/davidsdiaries
10. https://www.linkedin.com/pulse/stop-scroll-first-lines-adding-value-linkedin-news-posts-meadwell/
11. https://victressdigital.co.uk/are-webinars-dead
12. https://www.insidesales.com/twitter-for-business-prospecting/

CHAPTER FIVE

Designing Engagement and Interaction

The Key Takeaways

To build an engagement plan in a B2B social sales strategy, sales executives should focus on actively participating in conversations within their target industry by commenting on relevant posts, sharing valuable insights, and engaging with prospects' content.

This approach helps establish relationships and build credibility over time. Regularly interacting with influencers, decision-makers, and potential clients allows for meaningful connections that go beyond surface-level engagement. Prompt responses to comments and direct messages further demonstrate attentiveness and foster trust.

The goal is to create consistent, genuine interactions that nurture relationships and keep the brand top-of-mind, without appearing overly sales-driven. Don't push it.

Building an engagement and interaction plan is a crucial component of a B2B social sales strategy. In B2B sales, the goal is not just to promote your product or service but to establish meaningful relationships, build trust, and become a valuable resource for your target audience.

An effective engagement plan helps sales executives actively connect with prospects, influencers, and industry peers by fostering dialogue and demonstrating thought leadership.

Here's the key areas you need to focus on - how to build an engagement plan and maximize its effectiveness:

1. Actively Engage with Prospects and Influencers

This is your first stop. You know who your prospects are and who the key influencers are in your industry - talk to them without trying to sell anything.

For B2B sales executives, actively engaging with prospects and industry influencers is one of the most effective ways to establish a presence and nurture relationships. This requires ongoing participation in online conversations, commenting on posts, and sharing valuable content.

Commenting on Posts

Commenting on posts from prospects and influencers demonstrates that you're paying attention to their needs, insights, and challenges. Thoughtful comments also put your name in front of their audience, building visibility and credibility.

Avoid leaving generic comments like "Great post!" Instead, provide thoughtful feedback, additional insights, or ask open-ended questions. For example, if an influencer posts about new industry trends, you could comment with your own perspective or share a relevant resource.

Engage regularly with key accounts and influencers, building a rapport over time. Regular interaction helps keep you top of mind and fosters stronger connections.

Ensure your comments come across as authentic and personalized. Generic or promotional comments can appear insincere and may hurt your reputation.

For example, if a prospect posts about a challenge they're facing with supply chain disruptions, a B2B sales executive could comment, "This is a major concern right now, especially with ongoing global issues. We've seen companies implementing AI-driven solutions to streamline logistics. Have you considered using automation in any part of your process?"

Sharing Content from Prospects and Influencers

Sharing posts from prospects and influencers shows that you value their opinions and are willing to promote their work. It's a gesture that signals appreciation and collaboration.

When you share a post, add your own insights or commentary to the share. This makes the post more engaging for your audience and shows that you've thought critically about the content.

When sharing a post, tag the original author (e.g., @mention on LinkedIn or Twitter/X) to notify them of your engagement. This can spark a conversation and potentially lead to further interaction.

When sharing content, explain why it's relevant to your audience and how it relates to your industry or the challenges your clients are facing.

Be aware that not everyone posts regularly on LinkedIn so you may need to think about how to start a conversation that connects based on a shared interest - not whatever you are selling.[1]

For example, if an industry influencer posts a report on new manufacturing technologies, you could share it with your network, adding a comment like: "Exciting new developments in the world of manufacturing! We've already seen how AI and automation are transforming operations. Here's a great read on what's coming next. Thanks to [Influencer] for sharing!"

Participating in Relevant Discussions

By participating in discussions, whether in the comments section or in industry-specific groups (like LinkedIn Groups or Twitter/X chats), you position yourself as an active and informed member of the community.

Join industry-specific groups on LinkedIn or follow relevant hashtags on Twitter/X. These forums are often hubs for valuable discussions where you can meet prospects and influencers.

Offer insights, data, or case studies when participating in discussions. Demonstrating expertise builds trust and makes you a go-to resource.

Open-ended questions encourage dialogue and show that you are genuinely interested in others' opinions. This can lead to deeper discussions and stronger relationships.[2]

For example, in a LinkedIn group focused on supply chain management, a B2B sales executive might respond to a discussion on optimizing warehouse operations by sharing how a particular automation solution improved efficiency for one of their clients, sparking further conversation and interest.

Responding Promptly to Comments and Messages

Responding to comments and messages in a timely manner is critical for building trust, credibility, and relationships. Quick responses signal attentiveness and reliability, which are crucial for nurturing B2B relationships.

Timely responses demonstrate professionalism and show that you value the conversation and the person reaching out. Delayed or no responses can give the impression of disinterest or neglect, damaging your reputation and potentially losing prospects.

In fast-moving social media environments, prompt replies help maintain the momentum of conversations, keeping prospects and influencers engaged and deepening your connection.

Best Practices for Responding to Comments

Whether a comment is a compliment, question, or even criticism, make sure to acknowledge it. Ignoring a comment, even if it seems minor, can be seen as dismissive.

Don't just respond for the sake of it. Offer thoughtful, personalized replies that address the specifics of the comment. If a prospect asks a question, provide a detailed and relevant answer.

Keep the conversation going by asking a follow-up question or expanding on your response. This further engages the commenter and shows genuine interest.

Always maintain professionalism in responses, even if the comment is critical. Keep your tone polite and helpful, as this will reflect positively on your brand and personal image.

For example, if someone comments on your LinkedIn post about AI in manufacturing, asking, "How does this technology integrate with existing systems?", your response could be: "Great question! AI solutions are increasingly designed to integrate with legacy systems. For example, our clients have found that predictive maintenance tools can seamlessly connect with their ERP systems, reducing downtime. Have you considered this for your operations?"

Best Practices for Responding to Direct Messages

Messages, especially direct inquiries from prospects, should be responded to as soon as possible. A delay might result in the prospect losing interest or moving on to a competitor.

When responding to messages, be clear and concise while addressing the prospect's question or request. If the message requires a detailed response, offer to set up a call or meeting to discuss further.

Avoid sending generic responses. Tailor your reply to the specific question or context of the message to show that you've read and understood their inquiry.

Always aim to move the conversation forward by suggesting the next steps, whether that's a follow-up call, sending additional resources, or connecting with another relevant team member.

For example, if a prospect messages you asking about pricing for your solution, you could respond: "Thanks for reaching out! Pricing varies based on the size and needs of your operation, but I'd be happy to provide a detailed quote based on your requirements. Would you like to schedule a quick call to discuss your specific needs?"

Monitoring and Engaging with Industry Hashtags and Keywords

Using hashtags and following specific industry keywords can help you find and engage with relevant conversations in real time. This is particularly useful on platforms like Twitter/X and LinkedIn, where users actively discuss industry news, trends, and pain points.

Monitor Industry Hashtags

Identify and follow hashtags relevant to your industry (e.g., #supplychain, #manufacturingAI). Tools like Hootsuite or X Pro can help you track these in real time. You can also just type a hashtag directly into the search bar on LinkedIn.[3]

Engage with posts under these hashtags by commenting, liking, and sharing. Use your engagement as an opportunity to add value to the conversation or connect with prospects.

For example, if you're selling B2B software to the healthcare industry, following hashtags like #healthcareIT or #medtech can give you opportunities to engage with industry professionals and contribute to ongoing discussions.

Follow and Engage with Keywords

Track specific keywords related to your industry, products, or services. This can help you identify when prospects or influencers are discussing topics related to your solution.

It's also worth reviewing your own profile to make sure that all the keywords you think are relevant for your business are included on your profile - that is what other people will be looking for.[4]

Jump into conversations where your expertise is relevant. For instance, if someone is discussing the benefits of automation in their industry, offer insights on how your solution has helped other companies achieve similar goals.

Building Relationships Over Time

Social selling is about nurturing relationships over time, not just immediate conversions. To build lasting relationships with prospects and influencers, focus on consistency and value.

Engage Regularly

Don't just engage with a prospect or influencer once—continue the conversation over time. Regular interactions (liking posts, commenting, sharing updates) help keep you on their radar.

Use LinkedIn's "Notifications" feature to see when your key prospects or influencers are posting updates, and engage with them consistently.

Offer Value Before Asking for Anything

Focus on providing value to your prospects and influencers before asking for anything in return. Share helpful resources, offer insights, and engage in meaningful ways that demonstrate your expertise.

When the time comes to pitch your solution or request a meeting, they'll already see you as a trusted advisor, making them more likely to respond positively.[5]

Be Genuine and Authentic

Building authentic relationships is key to successful social selling. Avoid overly salesy or promotional language. Instead, focus on building real connections through genuine interest, thoughtful dialogue, and helpful contributions.

This can all seem overwhelming. You probably don't want to spend hours of each day on LinkedIn just thinking up comments for reports posted by influencers, but most of the people that are important to you - influencers and prospects should already be on your radar.

You just need to be more mindful about interacting and commenting - adding value to the discussion. Don't just lurk in the shadows following what everyone else is saying.

Building an engagement and interaction plan is essential for B2B sales executives to successfully leverage social media in their sales strategy.

By actively engaging with prospects and influencers through thoughtful comments, sharing relevant content, participating in discussions, and responding promptly to messages, sales executives can build trust, establish credibility, and foster meaningful relationships over time.

A consistent, authentic, and value-driven approach will enable sales teams to position themselves as trusted advisors, leading to deeper connections and stronger business outcomes.

References:

1. https://www.linkedin.com/pulse/how-engage-prospect-linkedin-even-dont-post-dean-seddon/
2. https://www.linkedin.com/pulse/how-do-i-make-linkedin-group-posts-work-me-mike-michael-/
3. https://sproutsocial.com/insights/linkedin-hashtags/
4. https://www.linkedin.com/pulse/zero-hero-linkedin-using-keywords-optimize-your-oscar-agudelo-/
5. https://www.linkedin.com/advice/0/how-do-you-balance-value-pitching-social-selling

CHAPTER SIX

Personal Branding

The Key Takeaways

Personal branding is vital for B2B sales executives in a social sales strategy because it helps differentiate them from competitors and builds trust with potential clients. By sharing personal insights, successes, and expertise, sales executives humanize the brand, making it easier for prospects to connect on a personal level.

A strong personal brand allows sales professionals to showcase their credibility, thought leadership, and industry knowledge, positioning them as trusted advisors rather than just salespeople.

This authenticity fosters deeper relationships with prospects and influencers, and when combined with a solid social presence, it enhances the overall sales strategy by creating lasting, meaningful connections.

Content marketing executives often mistake the need for content to be personal. Companies post endless blogs and whitepapers on their website "written by Brand X" and wonder why nobody is paying attention?

Nobody cares.[1]

Nobody looks online to see the latest insight posted on the Microsoft website, but if Satya Nadella posts a blog then it will get immediate attention.

Sales executives need to build their own profile. It may not be as significant as the Microsoft CEO, but they need to develop an online persona in their own field so the important prospects and influencers do know who they are.

This cannot be avoided. Building a strong personal profile for sales team executives is essential in B2B social sales strategy, as it helps humanize the brand and establish trust. By cultivating a robust personal brand, individual sales executives can strengthen their relationships with prospects, influencers, and decision-makers.

Here's how sales executives can develop their personal profile and why sharing personal insights, experiences, and successes is vital in building a connection with the audience.

Defining the Personal Brand

A personal brand is the image and reputation that a sales executive projects in their industry. For B2B sales, this brand should reflect both professional expertise and personal authenticity.[2]

Here's how to start defining and developing that brand:

Identify Core Strengths and Expertise

Sales executives should begin by identifying their strengths, expertise, and unique selling propositions (USPs). This may include specific industry knowledge, unique sales approaches, or success stories in helping clients solve challenges.

Focusing on a niche area within the industry allows executives to become recognized as experts in that domain. This could involve topics such as digital transformation, customer success, or product innovation within their field.

Ensure the personal brand aligns with the company's values and goals. Sales executives need to maintain a consistent message that reflects both their individual persona and the larger mission of the company.

Set Clear Objectives

Establish clear objectives for building a personal brand. This might include increasing visibility, building a larger network, generating leads, or being recognized as a thought leader in a particular area.

A personal brand takes time to develop. Executives should think of this as a long-term investment that will grow through regular, authentic contributions and engagement with the industry.

Creating and Sharing Personal Insights and Experiences

Sharing personal insights, experiences, and successes is essential to humanize the sales executive and make them relatable to the audience. Humanizing the brand helps build stronger emotional connections with prospects and key decision-makers.

Why Sharing Personal Insights Matters

Personal stories and experiences show authenticity and vulnerability, which help build trust with the audience. When executives share their challenges and lessons learned, it humanizes them and makes them more approachable.

Clients and prospects are more likely to connect with sales executives on a personal level when they share their experiences. A post about overcoming a tough sales challenge, for instance, can resonate with others facing similar obstacles.

Personal insights and experiences help differentiate individual sales executives from competitors. While everyone in the industry may have similar professional credentials, personal stories make the executive's journey unique. Telling personal stories really is just storytelling.[3]

An executive might share a post about how they helped a client implement a new technology, describing not just the technical details but also the emotions involved, such as the initial hesitation from the client and the eventual success.

Types of Personal Content to Share

Sales executives can share success stories about how they've helped clients achieve results. These stories should be framed not just as a promotional message but as a genuine narrative of collaboration, problem-solving, and positive outcomes.

Sharing the lessons learned from both successes and failures helps show humility and continuous improvement. This is particularly powerful for executives as it positions them as transparent and willing to grow.

Provide a glimpse into the day-to-day activities, such as attending conferences, meeting with clients, or preparing for presentations. This gives prospects a better understanding of who the person is beyond their sales role.

Sales executives can also share their reflections on trends, challenges, or key developments in the industry. This positions them as thoughtful leaders who are keeping up with or shaping the industry's future.

For example, a sales executive might write a post about attending an industry conference, sharing key takeaways and personal observations about the new trends shaping their industry. They can add a few insights on how they plan to use these learnings to help clients.

Establishing Thought Leadership

While personal stories help humanize a sales executive, thought leadership is essential for building professional credibility. Sales executives need to share high-quality content that addresses industry pain points and offers valuable solutions to position themselves as trusted advisors.

Creating Thought Leadership Content

Sales executives should focus on creating in-depth, high-quality content that provides actionable insights to the target audience. Examples include:

- Blog posts on industry trends and innovations.
- Whitepapers or guides that dive deep into specific challenges clients face.
- Case studies that outline how they solved a particular problem for a client.
- Videos or webinars that offer expert advice or share insights on emerging trends.

The content should be relevant to the prospect's needs and pain points. Sales executives should always focus on delivering value and actionable insights rather than just promoting their products or services.[4]

Use different types of content to engage various parts of the audience. For example, whitepapers or case studies might appeal to more analytical decision-makers, while videos or infographics might engage a wider audience.

Consistency and Relevance

Establishing thought leadership takes time, so it's crucial to consistently publish and share valuable content. Executives should aim to post regularly, engage with others' content, and build up their profile over time.

Thought leadership content should be highly relevant to the target audience's challenges and goals. Staying on top of industry trends and client needs ensures that the content resonates and stays valuable.

Engage in Conversations

Actively engage with prospects and influencers who comment on their posts. Engaging in conversations helps build relationships and reinforces thought leadership.

Sales executives should participate in discussions in industry groups or forums to offer insights and show they are part of the broader industry dialogue.

Building a Strong Social Profile

To ensure that a sales executive's personal brand and insights gain visibility, they need a strong and optimized social media presence. Platforms like LinkedIn, Twitter/X, and industry-specific forums are excellent places to establish this.

Optimize LinkedIn Profile

Create a headline that reflects the executive's expertise and value proposition. Instead of just listing their job title, executives can emphasize how they help clients or their area of specialization (e.g., "Helping manufacturers implement cutting-edge AI solutions").

The LinkedIn summary should offer a concise narrative about the executive's professional background, industry expertise, and the unique value they bring to clients. It should be written in a way that's both approachable and insightful.[5]

LinkedIn's "Featured" section can be used to highlight thought leadership content, such as blog posts, case studies, or speaking engagements.

Encourage clients or colleagues to provide LinkedIn recommendations. These serve as testimonials that enhance the executive's credibility.

Leverage Twitter/X or Other Networks

Twitter/X: For executives in industries that are active on Twitter/X, regular posting of relevant news, industry insights, and participation in conversations using hashtags can increase visibility.

Participating in niche industry forums or communities where prospects and peers engage in discussions can help build a reputation as a knowledgeable and helpful leader.

Consistency in Personal Branding Across Channels

Consistency is key in personal branding. Sales executives should ensure that their messaging, tone, and content are aligned across all platforms. Whether they are posting on LinkedIn, Twitter/X, or engaging in industry discussions, the personal brand should remain cohesive, showcasing both expertise and authenticity.

Unified Messaging

Ensure that the personal brand reflects the core values, expertise, and insights consistently across all social media platforms. This helps build a recognizable and trusted persona that prospects can connect with.

Avoid over-promotional language or posting only about the company's products. The key is to share valuable content and engage in authentic conversations.

Showcase Successes and Achievements

Sales executives should highlight their key successes to reinforce credibility and showcase their ability to deliver results.

Share client success stories and testimonials (with permission). This adds social proof to their profile and demonstrates their expertise in solving real-world challenges.

If an executive has been recognized by their company or industry, sharing this with their network can help boost their profile.

For example, a sales executive might post, "Honored to receive our company's Sales Excellence Award this year! I'm grateful to work with amazing clients who trust us to help solve their biggest challenges. Special thanks to my incredible team for their support in every project."

Building a strong personal profile is essential for B2B sales executives to engage with prospects, influencers, and decision-makers effectively. By defining a personal brand that highlights core strengths, sharing personal insights and experiences, and establishing thought leadership, sales executives can humanize the brand and build trust with their audience.

Sharing both professional expertise and personal stories helps create meaningful connections and differentiates them from the competition. Consistency, authenticity, and engagement are the pillars of a successful personal brand in B2B social sales.

References:

1. https://ucmarketing.co.uk/should-you-include-an-author-on-a-company-blog-post/
2. https://www.retorio.com/blog/personal-brand-ai-sales-training
3. https://www.pygio.com/the-power-of-storytelling-in-sales/
4. https://www.forbes.com/councils/forbesagencycouncil/2023/04/19/what-it-really-means-and-takes-to-become-a-thought-leader/

5. https://www.linkedin.com/business/sales/blog/profile-best-practices/17-steps-to-a-better-linkedin-profile-in-2017

CHAPTER SEVEN

How To Use Social Listening

The Key Takeaways

Social listening is a crucial component of a B2B social sales strategy because it enables sales executives to monitor conversations, trends, and mentions related to their company, industry, competitors, and key topics.

By using social listening tools, they can gather real-time insights about what their target audience is discussing, identifying potential pain points, opportunities, and engagement moments. This helps in tailoring content and interactions to address relevant issues, making outreach more timely and effective.

Social listening also aids in identifying influencers and decision-makers, allowing sales teams to engage with the right people at the right time, ultimately fostering stronger relationships and driving sales opportunities.

A social listening strategy is a critical part of a broader social sales strategy for B2B companies, as it allows sales executives to monitor, analyze, and engage with conversations that are relevant to their industry, brand, competitors, and potential customers.[1]

By gathering real-time insights from social media platforms, sales executives can make data-driven decisions, identify engagement opportunities, and proactively address customer pain points.

Here's how sales executives can create an effective social listening strategy, why it's important, and how to use social listening tools to drive success.

Importance of Social Listening in a Social Sales Strategy

Social listening is essential for B2B sales executives for several reasons:

1. **Understanding Customer Needs:** By monitoring what potential customers are saying about their pain points, challenges, and needs, sales executives can tailor their content and outreach to address these issues more effectively.

2. **Identifying Engagement Opportunities:** Social listening helps identify when prospects are discussing relevant topics, enabling sales executives to join conversations and build relationships at the right time.

3. **Tracking Competitor Activity:** Monitoring competitors' mentions and customer feedback provides valuable insights into their strengths

and weaknesses, allowing sales teams to position offerings more effectively.

4. **Reputation Management:** By tracking mentions of their company, sales executives can respond quickly to both positive and negative feedback, reinforcing the brand's presence and credibility.

5. **Trend Monitoring:** Social listening helps sales executives stay on top of industry trends, giving them an advantage when crafting their social content strategy or engaging with influencers.

6. **Building Trust and Relationships:** Engaging with prospects based on real-time information demonstrates that the sales executive is listening and responsive, helping build trust and establish long-term relationships.

The Key Steps to Building a Social Listening Strategy

1. Define Objectives and Key Metrics

Before implementing social listening, sales executives need to define clear objectives - what are you listening for anyway? Do you want to know what customers are saying about your company or do you want to listen for what prospects are saying? These objectives will guide the process and ensure the right data is gathered.

Some common objectives include:

- **Identifying potential leads:** Look for conversations or mentions that indicate a company or prospect might need your product or service.

- **Understanding customer sentiment:** Monitor how your audience feels about your brand, competitors, or industry-related topics.
- **Tracking brand awareness:** Measure how often and in what context your brand is mentioned online.
- **Monitoring competitor activity:** Gather insights about competitors' strategies, product launches, and customer feedback.

Once the objectives are clear, identify key performance indicators (KPIs) to track success. KPIs might include:

- The number of mentions of your company or product.
- Share of voice (how much your brand is mentioned compared to competitors).
- Sentiment analysis (whether mentions are positive, negative, or neutral).
- Engagement opportunities (the number of conversations you were able to join or convert into leads).

2. Identify Key Platforms and Channels

Sales executives should identify the social media platforms and channels most relevant to their audience and industry. Depending on the target audience, the most important platforms might include:

- **LinkedIn:** Ideal for B2B industries, as it's a hub for professionals, thought leaders, and companies.

- **Twitter/X:** Great for real-time conversations and industry trends - although as a general network it is losing reach.

- **Facebook:** Useful for monitoring broader discussions, especially for businesses with a more diverse audience.

- **Industry forums or Reddit:** Important for niche industries where discussions might happen outside of mainstream social media platforms.

- **YouTube and Podcasts:** Monitoring comments or mentions in multimedia content can reveal customer insights and trends.

- **Instagram and TikTok:** although these visual platforms are often less important for B2B sales, it can still be useful to monitor information such as customer sentiment and brand awareness here.[2]

3. Monitor for Specific Keywords and Mentions

A central aspect of social listening is tracking relevant keywords, phrases, and hashtags across these platforms.[3]

These keywords can be divided into several categories:

- **Company Mentions:** Track direct mentions of your brand name, products, or services. This allows you to respond to customer feedback, questions, or potential leads.

- **Competitor Mentions:** Monitor your competitors' brand names, products, and services to gain insights into their market positioning, customer sentiment, and potential gaps in their offerings.

- **Industry Keywords:** Identify keywords that are relevant to your industry or niche. This could include trends, pain points, or terms related to the challenges your target audience faces. For example, if your company provides SaaS solutions, track terms like "digital transformation," "SaaS solutions," or "cloud software."

- **Influencers and Thought Leaders:** Keep an eye on mentions from industry influencers or thought leaders who shape conversations in your field. This can help identify opportunities to engage with them or align your content with trending discussions.

Using these keywords, sales executives can stay ahead of important discussions and trends, which will inform their content creation and engagement strategies.

4. Use Social Listening Tools

Several social listening tools can help sales executives automate the process of monitoring mentions and gathering insights. Some of the most popular tools include:

- **Hootsuite:** This tool allows you to monitor mentions, keywords, hashtags, and industry trends across multiple platforms from a single dashboard. It's useful for tracking real-time conversations and scheduling posts.[4]

- **Sprout Social:** Provides in-depth analytics and social listening capabilities, allowing sales executives to track sentiment, brand mentions, and competitor activity.[5]

- **Brandwatch:** Offers detailed sentiment analysis, competitive intelligence, and audience insights by monitoring conversations happening around your brand and industry.[6]
- **LinkedIn Sales Navigator:** Specifically designed for LinkedIn, this tool helps sales executives track prospects, monitor mentions of key decision-makers, and find engagement opportunities on the platform.[7]
- **Mention:** This tool enables sales executives to track brand mentions, keywords, and competitor activity in real time across a variety of platforms, including news sites and blogs.[8]

Using these tools, sales executives can easily filter conversations based on the objectives set earlier and gather actionable insights for their social sales strategy.

5. Analyze the Data for Actionable Insights

Once data is gathered from social listening, sales executives must analyze it to extract valuable insights. These insights can inform various aspects of the social sales strategy:

- **Customer Pain Points:** Analyzing what customers are discussing and complaining about can help identify recurring pain points. Sales executives can then address these in their outreach, content, and product positioning.

- **Competitor Weaknesses:** By monitoring competitor mentions, sales teams can spot dissatisfaction among their customers, offering an opportunity to pitch an alternative solution.

- **Trending Topics:** Keep track of trending topics in your industry, so your content and conversations stay relevant. For example, if a new regulation is gaining attention, sales executives can craft posts or content to share expertise on the subject.

- **Audience Sentiment:** Track sentiment around your brand and adjust your messaging accordingly. If sentiment is negative, take steps to address concerns and engage with customers to resolve issues.

6. Engage Based on Insights

The real power of social listening comes from using the insights gained to engage with prospects and industry influencers.[9]

Sales executives should focus on:

- **Joining Conversations:** When a prospect mentions a problem that your company can solve, jump into the conversation by offering helpful insights or solutions. This demonstrates that you're listening and ready to assist.

- **Acknowledging Brand Mentions:** Respond promptly to both positive and negative mentions of your brand. Thanking customers for their praise or addressing concerns shows that you are responsive and committed to customer success.

- **Sharing Relevant Content:** Tailor your content based on the trends and conversations you've monitored. If your audience is frequently discussing a particular challenge, create content that offers valuable solutions, like blog posts, infographics, or videos.

- **Connecting with Influencers:** If an industry thought leader is discussing a topic relevant to your business, engage by adding your insights, sharing their content, or starting a conversation. This helps build relationships with influencers who can amplify your message.

7. Refine and Adapt the Strategy

Social listening is not a one-time activity. It requires continuous monitoring and adaptation to stay ahead of industry trends and audience needs. Regularly review the performance of your social listening efforts and refine the keywords, platforms, and engagement tactics based on new insights.

Example of Social Listening in Action

Let's say a sales executive works for a B2B software company that provides cloud-based solutions. Through social listening, they identify that a significant number of LinkedIn users are discussing challenges related to scaling their infrastructure. Many of these conversations mention competitors' products, but there is a growing frustration around the lack of flexibility in those solutions. The sales executive can:

- **Engage:** Join the conversation by acknowledging the challenge and offering insights into how their cloud-based solution can address flexibility concerns.

- **Create Content:** Develop blog posts or case studies that specifically highlight how their product provides more scalable and flexible options compared to competitors.

- **Follow-Up:** Use the conversation as an opportunity to directly engage with prospects, offering personalized solutions and demonstrations of the product.

Social listening is a powerful tool that allows sales executives to stay connected with their audience, competitors, and industry in real time. By monitoring social media platforms for mentions of their company, competitors, and relevant keywords, sales teams can gather valuable insights, identify engagement opportunities, and position themselves as trusted advisors.

Using social listening tools helps automate this process, making it easier to stay informed and agile in a fast-moving digital landscape. With a well-executed social listening strategy, B2B sales executives can build stronger relationships, respond proactively to customer needs, and ultimately drive better sales outcomes.

Don't be scared. This is a lot to take in and you can't monitor everything all the time. You don't need to follow absolutely all this advice, but just be aware that keeping an ear to the ground can help to trigger ideas.

The seven stages listed in this chapter will be difficult to implement for an individual sales executive without some administrative support, but at the very least ensure that your LinkedIn Sales Navigator is tuned in to what prospects, clients, and the competition are all saying.

Even a simplified listening strategy will allow you to create content or directly engage based on what people are saying in the marketplace.

References:

1. https://www.sprinklr.com/blog/b2b-social-listening/
2. https://www.emarketer.com/content/using-tiktok-b2b-marketing
3. https://www.linkedin.com/pulse/8-best-practices-b2b-social-listening-internet-tomasz-zduleczny
4. https://www.hootsuite.com/
5. https://sproutsocial.com/
6. https://www.brandwatch.com/
7. https://business.linkedin.com/sales-solutions
8. https://mention.com
9. https://thecmo.com/marketing-technology/mastering-social-listening/

CHAPTER EIGHT

Networking and Relationship Building

The Key Takeaways

A B2B social sales strategy helps build relationships and support networking by leveraging social media platforms to connect with key decision-makers, influencers, and prospects.

Through consistent, meaningful engagement—such as commenting on posts, sharing relevant content, and participating in discussions—sales executives can foster authentic connections over time. This strategy enables professionals to stay visible, establish trust, and demonstrate their expertise in a non-salesy manner.

By attending virtual events, webinars, and industry forums, salespeople can further expand their network, cultivating relationships that may evolve into business opportunities. Overall, social sales nurtures relationships in a way that traditional methods often cannot, creating lasting connections that benefit both parties.

Building a strong network and developing relationships is crucial for B2B sales executives in the digital age. LinkedIn and other online platforms offer vast opportunities to connect with potential clients, influencers, and industry peers, while virtual events and forums provide additional avenues for engagement and relationship-building.

It is also worth adding that even where you have an extensive network that was nurtured the old school way - over warm wine at conferences - you can stay closer to these existing connections by developing a stronger digital bond.[1]

How often are you really going to meet with that prospective customer in Reno, Nevada each year anyway? Instead of saying hello at an annual conference once a year, you can monitor what that prospect is talking about and get closer by engaging more regularly with them.

Here's how a sales executive can effectively expand their network and forge valuable connections through a strategic approach.

1. Building a Network on LinkedIn and Other Platforms

LinkedIn is the premier platform for B2B networking, and sales executives can leverage its tools to connect with potential clients, influencers, and decision-makers.

Here's a step-by-step guide to building a network on LinkedIn and similar platforms.

How Do You Look? Optimize Your LinkedIn Profile

Before reaching out to potential connections, it's essential for the sales executive to have a polished and professional LinkedIn profile. An optimized profile acts as a digital resume and a first impression.[2]

- **Headline:** Write a compelling headline that goes beyond a job title. Highlight your expertise and how you add value (e.g., "Helping SaaS Companies Scale with Cloud Solutions | B2B Sales Executive").
- **Profile Picture:** Use a high-quality professional photo. This increases the likelihood of getting accepted into people's networks.
- **Summary:** Craft a summary that tells your story, outlining your professional background, achievements, and how you can help your connections succeed. Focus on the value you bring to your network.
- **Skills and Endorsements:** Make sure your skills align with your target audience. Ask colleagues and clients for endorsements to boost credibility.

Identify Target Clients and Influencers

Sales executives should carefully identify whom to connect with, targeting two main categories: potential clients and industry influencers. To find them:

- **LinkedIn Search Filters:** Use advanced search filters to narrow down connections by industry, job title, location, and company size. For instance, if you're targeting CFOs in tech companies, use the filter to find CFOs in the desired vertical.

- **Explore Mutual Connections:** Leverage existing contacts to identify and reach out to secondary connections. A mutual contact provides credibility and can often lead to easier introductions.
- **Follow Companies and Industry Influencers:** Stay up to date with industry trends by following key companies and influencers. This allows you to engage with their content and make connections naturally.

Personalize Connection Requests

Sending generic connection requests is less effective. Instead, sales executives should craft personalized messages that demonstrate genuine interest and relevance.[3]

A good connection request:

- References common interests, groups, or industry events.
- Mentions a specific reason for connecting (e.g., "I saw you commented on a post about cloud solutions, and I'd love to connect and exchange insights on this topic.").
- Is respectful and not overly salesy. The initial goal is to build a relationship, not pitch a product right away.

Engage Consistently with Your Network

Once a sales executive has connected with potential clients and influencers, ongoing engagement is key to nurturing those relationships. Ways to engage include:

- **Comment on Posts:** Offer thoughtful comments on your prospects' and influencers' posts. Show you're knowledgeable and interested in the topics they care about.

- **Share Relevant Content:** Share valuable articles, insights, and industry news that align with your prospects' interests. When you come across content that may resonate with someone in your network, tag them in your post or message them directly with a note (e.g., "Thought you'd find this study on SaaS trends interesting!").

- **Engage with Thought Leaders:** Regularly interact with industry thought leaders by liking, commenting, and sharing their content. This increases your visibility and can lead to organic connections.

2. Participating in Virtual Events and Webinars

The rise of virtual events, webinars, and online forums presents a fantastic opportunity for sales executives to meet and engage with industry peers, potential clients, and influencers in real-time without geographical limitations.[4]

Here's how to make the most of these events.

Identify Relevant Events

Sales executives should seek out virtual events that align with their industry, products, and target audience. These can include:

- **Industry Conferences:** Many traditional conferences now offer virtual options. These attract key decision-makers, influencers, and industry leaders.

- **Webinars:** Look for webinars that focus on the pain points of your target audience or emerging industry trends. You can find these on platforms like LinkedIn, Eventbrite, or through industry associations.

- **Online Forums and Groups:** Platforms such as LinkedIn Groups, Reddit, and specialized industry forums are valuable for more casual yet impactful conversations.

Participate Actively in Virtual Discussions

Active participation is crucial to standing out in virtual environments. Sales executives can engage meaningfully by:

- **Asking Questions:** During webinars or virtual conferences, ask insightful questions during Q&A sessions. This can showcase your expertise and attract attention from both the speaker and the audience.

- **Contributing to Discussions:** In online forums or event chat rooms, contribute valuable insights or data points. If you notice a recurring theme, join the conversation with a helpful comment or link to a relevant resource.

- **Engage with Speakers and Panelists:** Follow up with speakers by sending them a message on LinkedIn, thanking them for their insights, and starting a conversation about the topics they discussed.

Host Your Own Virtual Events

In addition to attending events, sales executives can establish thought leadership by hosting their own virtual webinars or panel discussions.[5]

- **Co-host with Influencers:** Collaborate with industry influencers or thought leaders to host a joint webinar. This helps broaden your audience and taps into the influencer's network.

- **Invite Key Prospects:** Extend personal invitations to key prospects, positioning your event as an opportunity for them to gain valuable insights.

- **Record and Repurpose Content:** Record the event and share it on social media, LinkedIn, or YouTube to continue driving engagement even after the event concludes.

3. Using LinkedIn Groups and Industry-Specific Platforms

LinkedIn Groups and other industry-specific platforms provide a space for sales executives to connect with like-minded professionals and engage with prospects in a more focused environment.

Join and Contribute to Relevant Groups

LinkedIn Groups are niche communities where professionals gather to discuss industry trends, share challenges, and network. To leverage these groups:

- **Join Groups Aligned with Your Target Market:** Search for groups that attract your ideal clients and engage in discussions. For example, if you sell to financial services companies, join groups centered around banking technology or fintech innovation.

- **Add Value to Discussions:** Be active in the group by answering questions, sharing helpful resources, and starting discussions. Avoid overt selling and focus on contributing value.

- **Connect with Members:** After engaging in group discussions, send personalized connection requests to members you've interacted with. Reference your shared group or conversation in the connection message.

Engage with Industry-Specific Platforms

Some industries have dedicated online platforms or forums that serve as knowledge-sharing hubs. For example:

- **Quora and Reddit:** These platforms have industry-specific subforums where users discuss business challenges. Engage in relevant threads to showcase your expertise and connect with potential leads.[6]

- **Niche Networks:** Industries like healthcare, finance, and tech often have dedicated forums or networking sites where professionals gather to exchange insights and solutions.

4. Creating and Sharing Personal Insights to Humanize the Brand

In today's digital world, building relationships requires more than just sharing company-focused content. Sales executives should share personal insights, experiences, and success stories to humanize their brand and foster connections. Here's how:

- **Share Personal Stories:** Posting about your personal experiences—whether in sales, industry challenges, or customer successes—can make you more relatable and approachable.

- **Highlight Client Wins:** Share stories about how you helped clients overcome challenges, ensuring you focus on the value provided rather than a sales pitch.

- **Celebrate Milestones:** Share personal and professional milestones, such as new certifications, awards, or achievements. These posts often generate high engagement and help build rapport.

- **Leverage Video Content:** Videos showcasing your personality, insights, or advice can create stronger connections. They can be informal (such as a quick industry update) or more structured, like a video blog.

Building a network and establishing strong relationships are key components of a B2B social sales strategy.

It's all about the relationships. Are you inserting yourself into B2B conversations that demonstrate you know what you are talking about and can offer valuable ideas?

Sales executives can expand their network by optimizing their LinkedIn profiles, targeting the right connections, and engaging meaningfully with prospects and influencers.

Attending virtual events and contributing to online discussions on forums, groups, and webinars are additional ways to foster relationships and build thought leadership.

By sharing personal insights and engaging consistently, sales executives humanize their brand, making them more relatable and trustworthy. Social media, when used strategically, can be an invaluable tool for cultivating long-lasting, high-value B2B relationships.

References:

1. https://www.linkedin.com/pulse/getting-back-touch-old-contacts-ron-gibson/
2. https://www.linkedin.com/pulse/how-stand-out-linkedin-5-tips-boost-your-profile-talentfoot/
3. https://www.linkedin.com/pulse/dont-send-me-generic-invites-linkedin-anders-liu-lindberg/

4. https://www.linkedin.com/pulse/why-webinars-still-work-eric-siu--pqkxe/
5. https://www.goto.com/resources/how-to-create-and-host-a-webinar
6. https://www.fronetics.com/infographic-the-ultimate-guide-to-reddit-for-b2b-marketing/

CHAPTER NINE

Showing The Value Proposition

The Key Takeaways

A sales executive can use a B2B social sales strategy to inform prospects of their company's unique value proposition by sharing tailored content that addresses the specific needs and challenges of their target audience.

Through thought leadership posts, case studies, and success stories, they can highlight how their solution solves industry pain points while positioning their company as a trusted expert.

Engaging with prospects directly through comments, discussions, and personalized messages also allows the sales executive to communicate the company's value in a more personal, relevant way, making the interaction feel less like a sales pitch and more like valuable, problem-solving advice.

In building a B2B social sales strategy, clearly communicating the unique value proposition (UVP) of a product or service without coming across as overly focused on selling is critical. It requires balancing value delivery with personalization and genuine engagement, focusing on the needs of prospects rather than just pitching your product.

The following sections describe how a sales executive can effectively craft and communicate this message.

1. Focus on Value Over Features

When communicating your UVP, emphasize how your product or service solves real problems or creates opportunities for the prospect. Rather than leading with product features, highlight the outcomes or benefits the client will experience. This approach ensures that the focus is on adding value, rather than just pushing for a sale.

Helping is the new selling.[1]

2. Tailor the Message to Individual Prospects

One-size-fits-all messaging doesn't resonate in B2B sales. Personalizing your communication to each prospect shows that you've taken the time to understand their unique challenges and needs.[2]

To tailor your message:

- **Research the Prospect:** Use LinkedIn and other social media platforms to research their role, company, industry, and any recent updates or challenges they may be facing. Look for relevant news or case studies that reflect their situation.

- **Segment Your Audience:** Create different message frameworks for distinct customer segments (e.g., small businesses vs. enterprises, industries like healthcare or manufacturing). Address the specific pain points and goals of each segment, ensuring the content feels relevant.

- **Align Your UVP to Their Specific Challenges:** Once you understand their challenges, tweak your UVP to show how your solution specifically addresses those issues. For example, if you're reaching out to a healthcare company, highlight how your service improves patient management or regulatory compliance.

3. Position Yourself as a Problem-Solver

Rather than simply pushing a product, position yourself as a problem-solver and a trusted advisor. Approach your outreach from a perspective of helping the prospect overcome obstacles or achieve goals.

Ask questions to better understand their specific needs, and suggest solutions—even if that doesn't directly involve your product yet.

Examples of a Problem-Solving Approach:

- "I noticed your company is expanding into new markets. Many of our clients in similar situations have found that streamlining their supply chain with our tool has saved them significant time and

- reduced operational costs. Would you be interested in exploring how we could help you with this?"
- "I saw that you commented on a post about cybersecurity concerns in the finance industry. We've worked with several financial institutions to improve their security protocols, reducing risks and compliance issues. I'd love to share some insights if you're interested."

Offer ideas that make life easier for the prospective client. If you are offering a service that fixes their problem then 90% of the sale is already completed.[3]

4. Use Social Proof and Case Studies

People trust the experiences of others, especially in B2B sales where decision-makers want to see how similar companies have benefited from a solution. By using case studies, testimonials, and social proof, you can communicate your UVP in a way that demonstrates real-world results without appearing to be self-promotional.

- **Client Success Stories:** Share stories of clients who faced similar challenges and how your product helped them overcome these obstacles. Focus on measurable results like increased revenue, time savings, or improved efficiencies.
- **Industry-Specific Examples:** Tailor case studies to specific industries or sectors the prospect operates in. This increases relevance and credibility.
- **Client Endorsements:** Where possible, use client testimonials to back up your claims. Sharing a quote

from a satisfied customer can be more persuasive than touting your product's capabilities yourself.

5. Leverage Educational Content

Sales executives can use content like blogs, whitepapers, case studies, videos, and webinars to educate prospects rather than sell to them. By offering valuable insights and knowledge, you position yourself as a trusted resource.

Prospects are more likely to engage with educational content that addresses their needs, which opens the door to future sales conversations.

- **Content Addressing Pain Points:** Create or share content that speaks to the challenges your prospects face and demonstrates your understanding of their industry. For example, if you know a prospect is struggling with digital transformation, share an article or case study about how your solution has helped companies successfully navigate that shift.

- **Share Industry Trends and Insights:** Keeping prospects informed about the latest industry developments or market trends relevant to their business shows that you're in touch with the bigger picture. This adds value to your conversations and helps establish you as a thought leader.

6. Engage in Two-Way Conversations

Communication should not be one-sided. Instead of delivering a pitch, engage the prospect in a two-way conversation. Ask open-ended questions about their needs, priorities, and challenges.[4]

This not only helps you tailor your messaging but also builds trust by demonstrating that you're genuinely interested in their business and not just in making a sale.

Examples of Open-Ended Questions:

- "What challenges are you currently facing in scaling your team's operations?"
- "How are you navigating the transition to remote work, and are there any tools that could make the process smoother?"

By asking questions, you shift the focus from your product to the prospect's needs. This allows you to align your UVP naturally in response to their specific concerns.

This cannot be overstated. Instead of pitching a product or service, use your ongoing conversations to ask what they need.

7. Provide Value First

One of the most effective ways to communicate your UVP without appearing too focused on selling is by giving value upfront. Whether it's through offering insights, resources, or small favors, you can build goodwill that makes prospects more open to hearing your value proposition later.

- **Offer Free Resources:** Share a free guide, a tool, or access to a webinar that you know will help the prospect solve an immediate challenge. Even a personalized data report based on their industry can add value before the sales conversation begins.

- **Provide Expert Advice:** Without asking for anything in return, provide tailored recommendations based on your expertise. By offering solutions without an immediate sales pitch, you build trust and credibility.

A free consultation can be a very useful way to get noticed, but the advice needs to be insightful and useful - not just part of an obvious sales process.[5]

8. Tailor Your Follow-Up Messaging

Personalization should extend beyond the initial outreach. When following up with prospects, avoid generic messages. Instead, reference your previous conversations and offer new, relevant value in each interaction.

- "I remember we talked about improving efficiency in your customer service department. I just came across this case study that outlines some strategies you might find useful."

- "Based on our previous conversation, I've put together a quick analysis on how our product could improve your team's workflow. Let me know if you'd like to discuss."

9. Create Customized Sales Content for Key Prospects

For high-value prospects, creating custom content that addresses their unique needs and challenges can make a significant impact. This could include personalized reports,

ROI projections, or tailored case studies that speak directly to their goals.

- "Here's a custom analysis showing how your company could save 15% in operational costs by implementing our solution."
- "Based on our previous discussions, I've put together a case study that aligns closely with the challenges you're currently facing."

A successful B2B social sales strategy focuses on delivering value, addressing the unique needs of prospects, and building trust rather than merely pushing products.

By understanding the prospect's challenges and tailoring the communication of your unique value proposition, sales executives can foster meaningful connections that lead to long-term relationships.

Personalizing the message, providing educational content, and engaging in two-way conversations can ensure that your value proposition resonates while maintaining a customer-centric approach.

References:

1. https://www.marketlikeahuman.com/blog/helping-is-the-new-selling-why-adding-value-beats-pushing-sales
2. https://www.bol-agency.com/blog/3-reasons-why-b2b-personalization-essential-2024
3. https://www.marketsource.com/blog/five_problem-solving_tactics_turning_prospects_into_buyers/
4. https://www.indeed.com/career-advice/career-development/open-ended-questions-for-sales
5. https://abmatic.ai/blog/benefits-of-free-consultation-for-lead-generation

CHAPTER TEN

Lead Nurturing And Building A Pipeline

The Key Takeaways

A B2B social sales strategy can be used to build a pipeline of leads by consistently engaging with potential prospects on platforms like LinkedIn, where sales executives can connect with decision-makers and influencers in their industry.

By sharing relevant, high-quality content that addresses the challenges and needs of their target audience, they establish trust and attract interest from potential leads. Regular interaction, such as commenting on posts, participating in discussions, and sending personalized messages, helps nurture these relationships over time.

As prospects become more familiar with the sales executive's expertise and value proposition, they are more likely to move further down the sales funnel, converting into qualified leads.

Designing a B2B social sales strategy that effectively nurtures leads through the sales funnel involves a combination of targeted content and proactive engagement.

By using various content types to educate, engage, and guide prospects, and by leveraging tools like CRM systems to track interactions and manage follow-ups, sales executives can build a robust sales pipeline.

Here's how to approach this strategically.

1. Understanding the Sales Funnel in a B2B Social Sales Context

The sales funnel in B2B social sales includes the stages of awareness, interest, consideration, decision, and retention. The goal is to guide potential clients from initial awareness to making a purchase, while establishing long-term relationships.

As Paul O'Hara says in his foreword, you will not immediately see a pipeline full of business just because you started engaging with people on social networks. However, if you understand the pipeline then you can start using a social sales approach to building relationships that will become future partnerships.

Here's how a sales executive can align content and engagement strategies with each stage of the funnel.

Awareness Stage: Attract and Educate

At this stage, the focus is on creating brand awareness and engaging potential prospects who may not yet know about the sales executive's product or service. Content here should be broad, educational, and designed to capture interest.[1]

- **Content Strategy:** Share industry news, thought leadership articles, and insights related to industry challenges. Use blogs, social media posts, and videos that provide value without overtly promoting the product. Infographics and short videos can be effective for grabbing attention.

- **Engagement Strategy:** Engage by commenting on posts from industry influencers, sharing relevant third-party content, and participating in group discussions on LinkedIn. Build visibility through thoughtful interactions rather than sales pitches.

Interest Stage: Engage and Inform

Once prospects are aware of the brand, they may begin to show interest by following the sales executive's content or engaging with the company's social media presence. The focus here is to provide more detailed content that aligns with the prospect's pain points.

- **Content Strategy:** Offer whitepapers, webinars, and blog posts that dive deeper into how the product or service addresses specific industry challenges. Share case studies that demonstrate how similar companies have benefited from your solutions.

- **Engagement Strategy:** Interact with prospects who engage with your content—respond to comments, share additional resources, and reach out with personalized messages (e.g., "I noticed you liked our recent post on cloud computing trends—would you be interested in learning more about how we've helped companies in your industry?").[2]

Consideration Stage: Build Trust and Credibility

At this stage, prospects are evaluating their options and need more specific information about how the product or service can meet their unique needs.

- **Content Strategy:** Provide tailored content, such as ROI calculators, product demos, or customer testimonials that speak directly to the prospect's business challenges. Detailed case studies, comparison guides, and success stories can help build credibility.

- **Engagement Strategy:** Begin personalized, one-on-one outreach with prospects who show strong interest. Offer to answer specific questions or set up a call to walk them through how your product can solve their problems. The key is to be consultative and helpful, rather than overly aggressive.

Decision Stage: Support the Buying Decision

At the decision stage, prospects are ready to make a purchase decision but may need additional reassurance or support to close the deal.

- **Content Strategy:** Share pricing information, product demos, and implementation guides. Offer a clear value proposition with an emphasis on ROI, case studies, and testimonials that demonstrate the tangible benefits of the product or service.

- **Engagement Strategy:** Maintain close communication with prospects—schedule a product demo, offer tailored pricing, or provide any final pieces of information they may need. Ensure that the sales executive is readily available to answer questions or address concerns.

Retention Stage: Maintain Engagement Post-Sale

Once the sale is made, it's important to continue nurturing the relationship to encourage retention, cross-selling, and upselling.[3]

- **Content Strategy:** Share customer success stories, tips for getting the most out of the product, and updates on new features or offerings. Use newsletters and ongoing support content.

- **Engagement Strategy:** Regularly check in with the client, offer personalized support, and ensure they are satisfied with the product. Engaging with customers on social media and maintaining a dialogue can help foster long-term relationships.

2. Using CRM Systems to Track Interactions and Manage Follow-Ups

A Customer Relationship Management (CRM) system is essential for tracking interactions with leads, managing follow-ups, and nurturing relationships. It enables sales executives to stay organized, monitor the progress of leads through the funnel, and ensure timely and personalized outreach.

Benefits of Using a CRM in Social Sales

- **Centralized Data:** All interactions—whether they occur on social media, email, or during in-person meetings—are logged in the CRM. This gives the sales executive a comprehensive view of each prospect's journey.

- **Lead Scoring:** CRM systems often include lead scoring features, which help prioritize leads based on their level of engagement and likelihood of converting. For example, a prospect who has interacted with multiple pieces of content and attended a webinar would have a higher lead score than someone who simply liked a post. Lead scoring helps sales executives focus their efforts on the most promising prospects.

- **Automated Follow-Ups:** CRM tools allow sales teams to schedule and automate follow-up messages, ensuring that no lead is neglected. For instance, if a prospect downloads a whitepaper, the CRM can trigger a follow-up email or social media message offering further assistance or resources.

- **Personalization:** With detailed data on each prospect, a CRM enables more personalized communication. Sales executives can track what content a lead has interacted with, their specific pain points, and prior conversations. This allows them to tailor their outreach and offers based on the prospect's needs, increasing the chances of conversion.

- **Tracking Engagement Across Channels:** Social sales involve multiple touchpoints—LinkedIn, Twitter/X, email, webinars, and more. A CRM system consolidates all interactions into a single platform, allowing the sales team to see the bigger picture and analyze which strategies are most effective. Using CRM to Manage the Social Sales Process

- **Track Social Media Interactions:** Use CRM integrations with platforms like LinkedIn or Twitter/X to track when prospects engage with your posts or respond to outreach. These interactions can trigger automated follow-ups or alert sales executives to reach out personally.
- **Set Reminders for Follow-Ups:** Schedule follow-ups based on prior interactions. For example, if a prospect expressed interest but isn't yet ready to buy, a CRM can remind you to reach out in a few weeks or months.
- **Segment Prospects:** Use the CRM to segment leads based on factors like industry, job title, or level of engagement. This allows sales executives to create more targeted and effective social sales campaigns.[4]

3. Can Social Sales Build a Sales Pipeline?

Yes, a well-executed social sales strategy can significantly contribute to building a strong sales pipeline. It's not your only tool in the toolbox, but in the 2020s, a significant proportion of B2B sales activity needs to be in social sales.

Here's how it works:

Expanding Reach and Visibility

Social media platforms, particularly LinkedIn, allow sales executives to connect with a wide network of potential leads, industry influencers, and decision-makers. By consistently engaging and sharing high-quality, relevant content, sales executives can increase their visibility, making it easier for prospects to discover them.

Put yourself in the shoes of your prospects. How would you search for information on products or services in your industry?

- **Engagement Drives Leads:** Commenting on posts, sharing valuable content, and participating in industry-specific groups or forums helps establish a sales executive as a thought leader. Over time, this consistent presence attracts prospects and opens the door to new conversations.

- **Targeting Ideal Prospects:** LinkedIn and other platforms provide advanced targeting features that allow sales executives to connect with specific individuals based on their job title, industry, or location. This helps in focusing efforts on high-quality leads. Building Relationships

Social sales are centered around building trust and relationships, which is essential in B2B sales. Engaging consistently with potential clients over time creates a sense of familiarity and reliability, making them more likely to turn to the sales executive when they are ready to buy.[5]

- **Personalized Outreach:** Sales executives can develop rapport by offering helpful insights, answering questions, and engaging in genuine conversations with prospects. This personalized, human-centric approach contrasts with traditional cold outreach and makes prospects more receptive to further discussions.

- **Nurturing Leads Over Time:** Social media is an effective platform for nurturing leads who aren't ready to buy immediately. Through regular content sharing, engagement, and personalized follow-ups, sales executives can keep leads warm until they reach the decision stage.

Leveraging Social Listening for Insights

Social listening tools can help sales executives monitor mentions of their brand, competitors, and relevant industry topics. This data is invaluable for identifying engagement opportunities and trends that may inform future content and outreach strategies.

- **Identifying Pain Points:** By monitoring social media conversations, sales executives can gather insights into the common challenges and concerns prospects face. This allows them to create content that addresses those issues directly.
- **Engagement Opportunities:** Social listening tools alert sales teams to when prospects mention relevant industry topics or ask questions. This creates an opportunity to engage in real-time, offering solutions or insights that move the conversation toward a potential sale.

A successful B2B social sales strategy combines a mix of high-quality content and proactive engagement with the use of CRM systems to track and nurture leads. By aligning content strategies with each stage of the sales funnel—awareness, interest, consideration, and decision—sales executives can create meaningful interactions that build trust and foster relationships.

Implementing a CRM system ensures that no lead is lost, personalizes follow-ups, and tracks the effectiveness of social media interactions.

This holistic approach, when executed well, can transform social sales from passive engagement into an active, pipeline-building strategy, helping sales teams consistently generate and nurture leads toward successful conversions.

References:

1. https://www.linkedin.com/pulse/beginners-guide-using-linkedin-attract-right-people-your-klaver/
2. https://www.linkedin.com/pulse/b2b-prospecting-best-practices-getsalespipe-ccxbf/
3. https://www.touchpoint.com/blog/customer-retention-strategies/
4. https://docs.prospect365.com/en/articles/5316545-segmenting-your-customers-prospects
5. https://www.b2brocket.ai/blog-posts/why-relationship-building-is-important-in-the-b2b-sector

CHAPTER ELEVEN

Measurement and Analytics

The Key Takeaways

Success in a B2B social sales strategy can be measured by setting clear goals and tracking key performance indicators (KPIs) such as lead generation, engagement rates, and content performance.

Using analytics tools, sales executives can monitor metrics like the number of connections made, interactions on posts, and inbound inquiries resulting from their social activities. However, true success goes beyond just these metrics; it also includes the conversion of prospects into qualified leads and the growth of the sales pipeline.

Regularly reviewing data and adjusting the strategy based on insights ensures that social efforts are driving tangible business results rather than just generating vanity metrics.

Measuring the success of a B2B social sales strategy involves more than just setting goals and tracking metrics. While setting clear goals and KPIs is critical, the key lies in measuring both the activities that drive engagement and the actual business outcomes.

Here's a detailed look at how to approach this:

1. Setting Clear Goals and KPIs

The foundation of measuring success in any social sales strategy is setting clear, measurable goals and KPIs that align with broader business objectives. These goals should be specific, measurable, achievable, relevant, and time-bound (SMART).

However, it's important to go beyond setting basic engagement metrics like likes, shares, or comments. Ditch all the vanity metrics. What we want is relationships and sales, not thousands of likes from random people - or even just bots.[1]

Common Goals for B2B Social Sales:

- **Lead Generation:** How many qualified leads is the strategy bringing in?
- **Brand Awareness:** Are more potential clients aware of the company, its products, or services?
- **Sales Pipeline Growth:** Is the social strategy contributing to a larger and more engaged pipeline?
- **Customer Retention and Expansion:** Are current clients more engaged with the brand due to social selling efforts?

- **Revenue Contribution:** How much revenue can be directly attributed to the social sales strategy?

Key Performance Indicators (KPIs):

- **Engagement Metrics:** Likes, comments, shares, and clicks on posts. These metrics can be useful to compare how your content is landing, but don't ever think that these social media metrics are the same as actual sales success.

- **Conversion Metrics:** The number of social media followers who convert to leads, the rate of form submissions from social posts, or the percentage of webinar attendees sourced from social channels.

- **Content Performance:** Downloads of whitepapers, blog post views, video watch times, and case study engagement.

- **Pipeline Impact:** New leads, demo requests, or meetings booked as a result of social media interactions.

- **Sales Impact:** Revenue generated from social-sourced leads, the deal velocity of leads originating from social sales efforts, and the number of closed deals influenced by social media.

2. Using Analytics Tools to Measure Effectiveness

Analytics tools play a crucial role in measuring the effectiveness of social media activities and content performance. The key is to track the right data that directly links to business outcomes, not just vanity metrics.[2]

Social Media Analytics Tools:

- **LinkedIn Analytics:** Track post performance, engagement rates, and follower demographics to understand which content resonates best with the target audience.
- **Google Analytics:** Measure traffic from social platforms to the company's website, tracking behaviors like time on page, bounce rates, and conversions.
- **CRM Systems:** Integrate social media tracking with your CRM to follow the journey of social leads through the funnel. This helps in tying social engagement directly to business outcomes.
- **Social Listening Tools:** Tools like Hootsuite, Sprout Social, or Brandwatch can help monitor mentions, sentiment, and engagement across platforms, helping to assess brand awareness and conversations about the brand or products.

3. Adjusting the Strategy Based on Data and Insights

One of the most important aspects of measuring the success of a B2B social sales strategy is the ability to adjust tactics based on data and insights.

Social sales isn't a "set it and forget it" activity—success depends on continual learning and optimization. Often you will be able to sense this intuitively, rather than needing data.

How to Optimize Based on Data:

- **Content Performance:** If certain content types (e.g., videos or case studies) drive more engagement or conversions, adjust your strategy to create more of that content. Similarly, if certain posts are underperforming, analyze why and avoid those approaches in the future.

- **Timing of Engagement:** Analyze when your audience is most active on social media and schedule posts or interactions accordingly. If data shows higher engagement on certain days or times, this can significantly increase visibility.

- **Audience Targeting:** If engagement data shows that certain segments (e.g., job titles, industries) are interacting more than others, fine-tune targeting to focus on those prospects.

- **Lead Nurturing:** Use data to see which prospects are engaging the most with your social content. Adjust your outreach and follow-up strategy to focus more on these leads, as they may be further down the sales funnel.[3]

4. Focusing on Business Results, Not Just Metrics

To avoid the pitfall of measuring vanity metrics like likes, shares, or followers, focus on metrics that tie directly to business outcomes.

This can be a danger when marketing and sales teams share resource or systems. Everyone wants to be popular online and see that their articles are getting those likes, but if it does not translate into connections with real people and sales then maybe your advice is just popular with business school students.

Here's how to prioritize results-driven measurements:

Link Social Media Efforts to Sales Results:

- **Track Social-Sourced Leads:** Use a CRM system to track where leads originated, allowing you to attribute revenue to social efforts. For example, you can track when a LinkedIn conversation leads to a demo request or when a prospect first engages with a social post and then enters the sales pipeline.

- **Measure Lead Quality, Not Just Quantity:** A large number of leads from social media can be appealing, but the quality of those leads is what truly matters. Ensure that the social leads are being qualified and moving through the pipeline, not just entering it.

- **Track Conversion Rates:** Measure how many social media leads convert into paying customers, not just how many likes or comments your posts get. Conversion metrics provide a clear indication of whether social media is influencing business growth.

- **Track Revenue from Social Channels:** For companies with advanced tracking capabilities, it's possible to assign revenue values to social media efforts, tracking the direct impact on the bottom line.[4]

Avoiding Vanity Metrics:

- Vanity metrics, such as followers, likes, or impressions, may indicate reach but don't necessarily correlate with business impact. Instead, focus on metrics like conversions, lead quality, pipeline growth, and sales closed as a result of social media engagement.

5. Combining Qualitative and Quantitative Measures

While data and KPIs are crucial, don't overlook qualitative feedback. Understanding the sentiment behind the engagement or the depth of conversations can give a clearer picture of the real business value behind the numbers.

Are people actually talking to you because of your content? If you create one strong conversation with a prospect then it doesn't matter if that article only had a few likes.[5]

Qualitative Measures:

- **Customer Feedback:** Are prospects or existing clients referencing your social media content in conversations with the sales team?
- **Influencer Relationships:** How are relationships with industry influencers growing? Are they engaging with and amplifying your content?
- **Brand Sentiment:** How do your target audience and prospects perceive your brand based on your social selling efforts? Use social listening to gauge sentiment and adjust messaging accordingly.

Measuring the success of a B2B social sales strategy requires a balanced approach that combines goal-setting, the use of analytics tools, and continual optimization based on data and insights.

While engagement metrics can be useful, the true measure of success lies in linking social media efforts to tangible business outcomes, such as lead generation, pipeline growth, and revenue.

By tracking the impact of social media activities through CRM systems, monitoring content performance, and focusing on lead quality, sales executives can avoid vanity metrics and focus on real results.

Additionally, adjusting the strategy based on data insights ensures that the social sales strategy remains dynamic and responsive to the needs of the business and its prospects.

Don't lose sight of what you really want - it's not more likes.

References:

1. https://www.linkedin.com/pulse/measuring-b2b-social-media-success-beyond-likes-followers-onlyb2b-kqpgc/

2. https://sproutsocial.com/insights/social-media-analytics-tools/

3. https://sopro.io/resources/blog/b2b-lead-nurturing

4. https://www.linkedin.com/business/marketing/blog/social-media-marketing/social-media-advertising-driving-revenue-b2b

5. https://altitudemarketing.com/blog/the-role-of-customer-feedback-in-refining-b2b-marketing-tactics/

CHAPTER TWELVE

Training and Empowerment

The Key Takeaways

Sales executives can be trained to engage in a B2B social sales strategy by developing their understanding of the key platforms where potential business clients engage, such as LinkedIn. Training should emphasize building a professional and credible online presence, identifying and connecting with decision-makers, and nurturing relationships through personalized, value-driven content.

Executives should be equipped with skills to listen to and understand client pain points using social listening tools and engage in meaningful conversations that position their company as a trusted solution provider. Continuous learning on trends, consistent follow-up, and leveraging analytics to optimize outreach are also critical for long-term success in B2B social selling.

When starting a B2B social sales strategy, it's crucial to provide sales executives with the right training, tools, and confidence to engage effectively on social media. Social selling requires a nuanced approach that blends traditional sales skills with modern digital techniques.

Training in social selling techniques and best practices, combined with empowerment through tools and resources, will be key to making sales executives feel confident in sharing their opinions and engaging with prospects.[1]

There is a tendency to assume that sales executives must know what they need to do - everyone knows how to use social media! For an individual salesperson in a small business, there may be no choice other than finding new ideas and strategies from YouTube and resources such as this. For a larger, more coordinated team, it will pay to think about some guidance and training so the entire team can be more coordinated.

Here's how you can approach training and empowerment for your team:

1. Essential Training for Social Selling Techniques

Training is the foundation for a successful social selling strategy. Sales executives need to understand not only how to use social media but how to leverage it strategically for sales.[2]

Key Areas for Training:

- **Social Selling Fundamentals:** Sales executives should receive a foundational understanding of social selling, including how it differs from traditional sales methods and why it's effective for B2B selling.

This will cover how to build relationships and trust rather than hard selling.

- **Platform-Specific Training:** Since LinkedIn is the dominant platform for B2B social selling, training on how to navigate LinkedIn (and other platforms) effectively is crucial. This includes optimizing profiles, using LinkedIn Sales Navigator, joining relevant groups, and engaging with influencers and prospects.

- **Content Creation and Curation:** Train the team on how to create and curate relevant content that resonates with their audience. This includes sharing industry news, commenting on trends, and posting thought leadership content. Teaching them how to align content with various stages of the buyer's journey is essential for nurturing leads.

- **Engagement Best Practices:** Provide guidance on how to engage with prospects by liking, sharing, commenting, and messaging. Sales executives need to know how to approach conversations in a consultative, helpful way rather than directly pitching. Role-playing and real-life examples can be useful for practice.

- **Personal Branding:** Training should focus on how to build a personal brand that aligns with the company's values but also shows individuality. Sales executives need to be comfortable sharing personal insights, experiences, and successes to humanize their approach while maintaining professionalism.

2. Empowering Sales Executives to Post Opinions and Views Online

One of the biggest challenges in social selling is empowering sales executives to feel confident enough to post their own opinions and views online.

Many executives have been taught that any public statements linked to the company must go through marketing first. They need to be given the ability to post comments, ideas, and opinions without the fear of feeling that they might say something stupid online.

I once messaged a client who provides technology to contact centers because one of their sales leaders had posted a meme of a French presidential candidate winking "about their contact center strategy" - in the middle of the French presidential election of 2024. I found out that nobody realized who was in the video.

So, disasters can happen, but think about how to minimize the risk and give people confidence to talk about the industry they work in without feeling they need to only ever publish "official" messages.

Leaders need to lead and show they are ready to share their views if they want the sales team to follow. But remember that sharing your opinion should still be focused on creating value.[3]

This requires a balance of training, trust, and encouragement from leadership.

Building Confidence Through Encouragement and Support:

- **Create a Safe Environment:** Encourage a culture where team members feel comfortable sharing their thoughts without fear of judgment. This can be supported by leadership actively participating in social selling, showcasing that sharing views and insights is valued.

- **Start with Structured Content:** To ease sales executives into sharing their own content, begin by having them share company-created content. Gradually, encourage them to add personal commentary or insights to those posts.

- **Provide Content Templates:** Offer pre-written content or templates that sales executives can customize and post. This gives them a foundation to work from, making it easier to start contributing on social media.

- **Content Review System:** Initially, provide a review process where sales executives can submit their posts for feedback from marketing or social media experts. This helps build their confidence by ensuring their posts are on-brand and effective.

- **Showcase Examples:** Highlight successful social selling examples from within the team or industry peers. When sales executives see their colleagues generating results from social selling, they are more likely to engage themselves.

3. Providing Tools and Resources for Effective Social Selling

Equipping sales executives with the right tools and resources is critical for efficient and effective social selling. Tools streamline engagement, tracking, and content management, making it easier for sales executives to stay active and relevant.

Essential Tools and Resources:

- **CRM Integration with Social Media:** Ensure that the sales team has access to a CRM system that integrates with social media platforms like LinkedIn. This allows them to track interactions, monitor leads, and follow up seamlessly.

- **Social Listening Tools:** Provide tools like Hootsuite, Sprout Social, or LinkedIn Sales Navigator to monitor conversations about relevant industry topics, competitors, and your brand. Social listening tools can also highlight opportunities for engagement.

- **Content Libraries:** Create a repository of pre-approved content that sales executives can share or modify, including blog posts, whitepapers, case studies, infographics, and videos. This ensures they always have high-quality, relevant content at their fingertips.

- **Content Scheduling Tools:** Tools like Buffer or Hootsuite allow sales executives to schedule posts in advance, making it easier for them to maintain a consistent presence on social media without having to post in real-time.

- **Analytics Tools:** Equip sales executives with access to analytics tools that help track the performance of their posts and engagement. Seeing measurable results, such as the number of leads generated or engagement rates, can motivate them to continue contributing.[4]

4. Continuous Learning and Adaptation

Social selling is an evolving discipline, so training and support need to be continuous. Regular updates on the latest best practices and tools will help your sales team stay ahead of trends and adapt their strategy as needed.

Ongoing Learning Opportunities:

- **Workshops and Webinars:** Organize regular workshops or webinars that focus on advanced social selling techniques, new platform features, or case studies of successful social sales strategies.
- **Peer Learning:** Encourage team members to share their experiences and results with each other. Peer success stories can serve as inspiration and learning tools for others.
- **Feedback Loops:** Create a system where sales executives can share feedback on what's working or where they feel stuck. This open feedback can inform future training needs and help the team improve collectively.

There is also a large amount of online content that is available free, or at a low cost, and is entirely focused on help and advice around social sales. Look at LinkedIn Learning[5] or Udemy[6] for examples and find what works for you and your team.

5. Encouraging Thought Leadership and Personalization

Sales executives should be encouraged to establish themselves as thought leaders by sharing their knowledge, expertise, and unique perspectives. This helps to humanize the brand and build trust with prospects.

Steps to Empower Thought Leadership:

- **Personal Insights and Experiences:** Encourage sales executives to share personal success stories, challenges they've faced, and lessons they've learned in their professional journey. This makes them more relatable and positions them as trusted advisors.

- **Active Participation in Industry Discussions:** Sales executives should be encouraged to join relevant LinkedIn groups, comment on posts from influencers, and participate in discussions. Engaging in conversations rather than just sharing content establishes them as thought leaders.

- **Be Authentic:** Encourage authenticity in their posts. Prospects are more likely to engage with real, relatable content than with corporate or overly polished posts.

Building a B2B social sales strategy requires equipping sales executives with the training, tools, and confidence to succeed.

Training in social selling techniques, including platform-specific strategies, content creation, and engagement best practices, forms the foundation. Empowering team members to share their opinions and insights through structured support, templates, and examples helps them feel comfortable engaging online.

Additionally, providing them with the right tools—such as CRM integration, social listening platforms, content libraries, and analytics tools—ensures that they can engage effectively and measure their impact. By fostering a culture of ongoing learning, support, and encouragement, sales executives can build personal brands that align with the company's goals while humanizing the brand and driving business outcomes.

References:

1. https://blog.hubspot.com/sales/social-selling-training
2. https://sproutsocial.com/insights/b2b-social-media-strategy/
3. https://hbr.org/2018/03/the-b2b-elements-of-value
4. https://www.ruleranalytics.com/blog/online-marketing/b2b-marketing-tools/
5. https://www.linkedin.com/learning/
6. https://udemy.com/

CHAPTER THIRTEEN

Collaboration with Marketing

The Key Takeaways

Sales executives can collaborate effectively with their marketing colleagues in designing a B2B social sales strategy by aligning their goals, insights, and messaging. By working closely with marketing, sales teams gain access to valuable customer data, audience segmentation, and targeted content that can be used to nurture leads and engage potential clients.

Marketing can support sales by creating personalized, relevant content that addresses specific client needs, while sales can provide feedback on client interactions and pain points to refine marketing strategies. This partnership ensures a cohesive approach to outreach, leveraging marketing's brand awareness efforts with sales' direct engagement for a seamless buyer journey.

Operating a B2B social sales strategy in partnership with the marketing team is critical for creating a cohesive and effective approach to attracting and nurturing leads. Aligning sales and marketing efforts ensures that both teams are working towards the same goals and leveraging each other's strengths to drive business results.

This all naturally makes sense, but the silos are strong in some companies. Some marketing teams are focused on brand visibility and care little about actually closing a deal. Both your sales and marketing teams will benefit from aligning on some shared values and building a coordinated strategy - especially if the sales team starts posting content online.

Here's how to ensure a strong collaboration between sales and marketing in a B2B social sales strategy:

1. Importance of Aligning Sales and Marketing Efforts

Aligning sales and marketing is essential for a cohesive approach that nurtures leads throughout the entire customer journey, from awareness to conversion.

When sales and marketing teams work in isolation, the messaging can become disjointed, and the customer experience may suffer.

Collaboration ensures that both teams are contributing to the same goals, using consistent messaging, and supporting each other's efforts.[1]

Benefits of Alignment:

- **Unified Messaging:** Consistent brand messaging across both sales and marketing builds trust with prospects and customers. Marketing provides the overarching brand voice, while sales personalizes and tailors that messaging to specific prospects.

- **Better Lead Quality:** When marketing and sales align, they can jointly define what constitutes a high-quality lead. This helps marketing generate more qualified leads, and sales can focus their efforts on prospects who are more likely to convert.

- **Efficient Lead Nurturing:** Marketing can handle the top of the funnel activities (awareness and engagement), while sales can take over with more personalized outreach as leads move further down the funnel. Collaboration ensures a seamless transition from marketing engagement to sales outreach.

- **Optimized Content Creation:** Marketing and sales can collaborate to create content that resonates with prospects at each stage of the buyer's journey. Sales teams provide insight into customer pain points, which helps marketing create relevant and impactful content that addresses those needs.

2. Sharing Insights and Feedback Between Sales and Marketing

A continuous feedback loop between sales and marketing is crucial for refining strategies, improving content quality, and enhancing the effectiveness of the social sales strategy.

Both teams bring unique perspectives, and sharing insights helps both to better understand the customer and fine-tune their approach.

If the teams have been historically separate then it may require strong leadership to encourage information sharing. However, if they can share ideas then the advantages of collaboration should be obvious.

For example, it should be clear to the marketing team that their role is to support the sales effort and the sales team should be seen to be working with marketing to ensure their work is valued. Each has to help the other.

How to Foster Insight Sharing:

- **Regular Collaboration Meetings:** Schedule regular meetings between sales and marketing teams to discuss results, share feedback, and review the performance of social media campaigns. Sales can provide insights into what types of messaging resonate with prospects, while marketing can share data on content performance.
- **Customer Feedback from Sales:** Sales teams have direct conversations with prospects and customers, so they are well-positioned to share feedback on common pain points, objections, and challenges. This feedback can help marketing create more targeted and relevant content.
- **Content Usage Insights:** Sales should share data on which pieces of content (e.g., case studies, whitepapers) are most useful during conversations

with prospects. If certain content is particularly effective at moving prospects through the funnel, marketing can create more of that type of content.

- **Marketing Analytics and Reports:** Marketing teams can share detailed reports on the performance of social media campaigns, including engagement metrics, click-through rates, and lead generation data. This helps sales teams understand which topics and formats are resonating with the audience.

3. Joint Development of a Content Strategy

A key area where sales and marketing collaboration is essential is in the development of a content strategy for social sales. Both teams can contribute to creating high-quality, relevant content that addresses the needs of the target audience and drives engagement.

Steps for Joint Content Development:

- **Sales Insights for Content Creation:** Sales teams can share firsthand knowledge of customer pain points, questions, and objections. This information helps marketing create content (such as blog posts, videos, case studies, and whitepapers) that addresses these specific issues.

- **Marketing Expertise for Content Production:** Marketing has the expertise to produce polished, professional content that reflects the brand voice and provides value to the audience. They can take the insights from sales and turn them into well-crafted content pieces.

- **Content Alignment with the Sales Funnel:** Marketing and sales should collaborate to map out the buyer's journey and develop content that aligns with each stage. For example, marketing may create educational content for the awareness stage, while sales may provide more in-depth case studies or product comparisons for the consideration stage.

- **Personalization Support:** Marketing can provide customizable content templates that sales teams can personalize for specific prospects or industries. This helps maintain consistency while allowing sales executives to tailor messaging to individual prospects.

4. Coordinating Campaigns for Maximum Impact

A successful B2B social sales strategy often involves coordinating specific campaigns that both sales and marketing can support. This could include product launches, promotional events, or thought leadership campaigns that require a joint effort to maximize reach and engagement.

How to Coordinate Campaigns:

- **Shared Campaign Goals:** Marketing and sales teams should work together to define the goals of each campaign, ensuring alignment on what constitutes success (e.g., lead generation, brand awareness, or customer engagement).[2]

- **Joint Promotion Efforts:** Marketing can create broader campaigns (e.g., social media ads, webinars, or email marketing) to generate awareness, while sales can engage directly with prospects who interact with those campaigns. For example, if marketing runs a webinar, sales can follow up with attendees to move them down the funnel.

- **Cross-Promotion of Content:** Sales teams can share marketing-created content (such as blog posts or infographics) on their personal LinkedIn profiles, while marketing can amplify the personal thought leadership content created by sales executives through company channels.

- **Event Collaboration:** Marketing and sales can work together to promote virtual or physical industry events, with marketing handling event promotion and sales focusing on engaging with attendees before, during, and after the event.

5. Providing Sales Teams with Marketing Tools and Resources

Marketing can empower sales teams with tools and resources that make it easier for them to engage effectively on social media. This includes not only content but also technology and platforms that enable social selling.

Key Tools and Resources:

- **Content Libraries:** Marketing can create and maintain a content library of blog posts, case studies, infographics, videos, and other assets that sales teams can easily access and share on social media. These resources ensure that sales executives always have relevant, high-quality content at their disposal.

- **Social Selling Playbooks:** Marketing can create playbooks that outline best practices for social selling, including guidelines for posting, engaging with prospects, and sharing content. Playbooks help ensure consistency across the sales team while giving them flexibility to personalize their approach.

- **Analytics and Reporting:** Marketing can provide sales teams with access to social media analytics tools and reports that track the performance of posts, campaigns, and interactions. This helps sales executives understand which content is working and which strategies need adjustment.

6. Co-Ownership of Metrics and Results

To truly align sales and marketing, both teams need to take shared ownership of the metrics and results that come from social sales activities.[3]

This creates a sense of collaboration and accountability, rather than viewing social selling as a siloed responsibility of one department.

Shared KPIs:

- **Lead Quality and Volume:** Both sales and marketing should be aligned on what defines a qualified lead and work together to ensure that social sales activities generate the right volume of high-quality leads.
- **Content Engagement:** Measure how well content is performing across both marketing and sales efforts. Are prospects engaging with social media posts, downloading content, and responding to calls to action?

- **Revenue Impact:** Ultimately, the success of social sales should be tied to revenue generation. Both marketing and sales should track how social activities contribute to the pipeline, deal velocity, and closed deals. This is the bottom line for everyone on the team - are we selling more?

A successful B2B social sales strategy requires close collaboration between the sales and marketing teams. Aligning their efforts ensures that both teams are working toward the same goals with consistent messaging, while leveraging each other's strengths to drive business outcomes.

Sales and marketing can share insights and feedback to refine strategies, improve content quality, and create a more seamless experience for prospects.

Together, they can develop a content strategy that aligns with the buyer's journey, coordinate campaigns for maximum impact, and measure shared success through key metrics.

By working in partnership, sales and marketing can create a powerful and cohesive approach to B2B social selling that delivers real results.

References:

1. https://www.salesforce.com/ca/hub/marketing/marketing-sales-b2b
2. https://www.bol-agency.com/blog/sales-and-marketing-alignment-for-b2b-success
3. https://fastercapital.com/topics/developing-shared-goals-and-metrics-for-sales-and-marketing-teams.html

CHAPTER FOURTEEN

Consistency and Persistence

The Key Takeaways

Consistency is crucial in a B2B social sales strategy as it builds trust, credibility, and recognition with potential clients. Regular, meaningful engagement through consistent messaging, content sharing, and interactions helps establish a brand's authority and keeps it top-of-mind for decision-makers.

Inconsistent efforts can lead to missed opportunities, erode trust, and make it harder to build lasting relationships. Consistency also allows for the collection of data over time, enabling sales teams to refine their approach based on what resonates most with the target audience, ensuring a sustained and strategic presence in the marketplace.

Maintaining a consistent presence on social media is crucial to building a successful B2B social sales strategy. Consistency helps sales executives stay top of mind with prospects, build trust, and establish credibility over time.

However, it's equally important to balance persistence with respect for prospects' boundaries to avoid coming across as pushy or intrusive.

Here's how to maintain a consistent presence while being respectful and non-intrusive:

1. Importance of Consistency in Social Selling

Consistency is key to ensuring that your brand and message are visible and recognizable to your target audience. In B2B sales, the buying cycle can be long, and prospects often need multiple touchpoints before they're ready to engage or make a decision. A consistent presence keeps you relevant, builds familiarity, and positions you as a reliable thought leader.[1]

Reasons That Consistency is Critical:

- **Staying Top of Mind:** Regular interactions and content help keep your brand and offerings in front of prospects. Even if they aren't ready to buy immediately, consistent engagement increases the likelihood that they'll think of you when the time is right.

- **Building Trust and Credibility:** Posting high-quality, relevant content consistently demonstrates expertise in your industry. Over time, this builds trust with your audience as they view you as a knowledgeable and reliable resource.

- **Engaging with New Prospects:** Social platforms like LinkedIn often expand your reach through engagement. The more consistently you post and interact, the more likely your content will appear in front of new, relevant prospects.

- **Adapting to Buyer Journeys:** Different prospects will be at various stages of their buyer's journey. A consistent presence ensures that you're available when they need information or are ready to engage.

It is also noticeable that many executives are not consistent. They may have a burst of activity online and then they are "too busy" for several months. Posting some content is better than nothing, but long delays may in fact mean that you are starting from the beginning each time.

2. Being Persistent While Respecting Boundaries

Persistence in social selling is important for building relationships, but it must be done thoughtfully to avoid overwhelming or alienating prospects. Respect for prospects' boundaries and preferences is crucial to maintaining a positive relationship.

I personally don't allow my name to be tagged in LinkedIn because I found that people would persistently tag me in their posts. I'm happy to join in a discussion, but I do not want to receive notifications every single time a contact posts online.

You need to judge the boundaries of your prospects and influencers. Some will want to be alerted to your latest content. Some will prefer to only engage occasionally.[2]

Balancing Persistence and Respect:

- **Monitor Engagement Signals:** Pay attention to how prospects engage with your content. If they like, comment, or share your posts, that's a signal they're interested, and you can increase your engagement with them. If a prospect seems disengaged, pull back a bit and give them space.

- **Timing and Frequency:** Be mindful of how often you're reaching out or posting content. Posting too frequently or bombarding prospects with messages can come across as pushy. A good rule of thumb is to ensure your content provides value and aligns with their needs rather than pushing a sale.

- **Respect Personal Preferences:** If a prospect has communicated their preferred way of being contacted or engaged, honor that preference. For example, some prospects may prefer engaging through comments on posts, while others may respond better to direct messages.

- **Focus on Value, Not Sales:** Ensure that your interactions and content are focused on delivering value rather than pushing for a sale. By sharing helpful information and addressing their challenges, you build a positive relationship without being overbearing.

3. Publishing Consistent Content Without Annoying Prospects

A key concern in social selling is how to stay consistent without overwhelming or annoying your audience. Striking the right balance between staying active and avoiding over-posting is essential for maintaining engagement.

Best Practices for Posting Content Regularly:

- **Content Scheduling and Variety:** Use a content calendar to schedule regular posts without overloading your audience. A well-planned mix of content types—blogs, infographics, videos, and industry news—ensures that you're providing value without becoming repetitive. For example, post 3–4 times a week rather than every day.

- **Quality Over Quantity:** Focus on the quality of your posts rather than how often you post. High-quality, insightful content that addresses your audience's needs and challenges will resonate more than a flood of low-value content.

- **Tailor Content to the Audience:** Ensure that the content you share is relevant to your prospects. Personalizing posts or messages to fit the interests and needs of your target audience helps maintain engagement without being intrusive.

- **Use Analytics to Optimize Posting:** Track how your audience is responding to your posts using social media analytics tools. This will help you determine the optimal frequency and content type. If you notice engagement dropping off, it may be a sign to adjust your approach.

Each individual needs to find their own preferred cadence, but in my experience most executives can be highly effective in a social environment sharing one or two news stories each day, possibly one original article each week, and taking 15-20 minutes to scroll their newsfeed commenting on other articles that have been shared.

You need to judge how your network responds to content being shared at the weekend. Some executives want to ignore their social media entirely because they are busy with their family. Others use the weekend as a time to catch up on less urgent tasks. Judge how your own network responds to your "Sunday Wisdom" posts.[3]

4. Engaging Without Being Overbearing

A critical component of social selling is engaging directly with prospects and influencers through comments, likes, and messages. While it's important to engage regularly, it's also essential to avoid over-engagement that may seem intrusive.

How to Engage Effectively:

- **Engage Authentically:** When commenting on posts or replying to messages, make sure your responses are thoughtful and add value to the conversation. Avoid generic comments like "Great post!"—instead, offer insights, ask questions, or share relevant experiences.
- **Respect the Prospect's Space:** If a prospect doesn't respond immediately, don't follow up too quickly or frequently. Give them time to engage on their own terms, and try to gauge their level of interest based on their responses.
- **Vary Interaction Types:** Instead of only sending direct messages or commenting on every post, mix up your engagement. Share their content, join

discussions in industry groups, or offer to help with a resource without directly pushing your product.

Be aware that it can come across as invasive if you are commenting 'what a fantastic post' on everything that your prospect ever posts online. Don't be a stalker. It is enough of a compliment to engage seriously with a post, rather than just posting a series of clapping hands.[4]

Add value in your comments and show that you understand what they are saying, rather than showering them with fake - and endless - praise.

Authenticity is the key here. You want to build a rapport and start a conversation. Telling someone they made an awesome post once sounds like praise. Telling them the same thing each time they make a post sounds like you have a bot auto-responding to anything your prospects are posting.

5. Leveraging Content to Stay Consistent and Valuable

To maintain a consistent social media presence, sales executives can use a variety of content formats to engage prospects without appearing too sales-driven. Mixing content types helps keep your presence fresh and interesting for your audience.

Types of Content to Share:

- **Educational Content:** Share blogs, whitepapers, or industry reports that educate your audience on relevant topics. Position yourself as a source of valuable information rather than a salesperson.

- **Case Studies and Success Stories:** Share stories that demonstrate how your product or service has helped other clients. Frame these stories in a way that highlights the challenges and solutions rather than directly pitching your product.

- **Industry News and Insights:** Sharing relevant industry news and trends positions you as someone who is knowledgeable and up-to-date on the latest developments in your field.

- **Personal Insights:** Occasionally share personal experiences, success stories, or lessons learned. This humanizes your presence and helps build a personal connection with your audience.

Be aware that if you are pre-programming LinkedIn to share some news stories in advance then the news agenda may change. There is no point scheduling a breaking news story to appear on your LinkedIn feed a week from now.

A B2B social sales strategy relies heavily on maintaining a consistent and visible presence on social media platforms, but it's equally important to do so in a way that respects prospects' boundaries and preferences.

Sales executives should focus on delivering value through high-quality content, thoughtful engagement, and personal connections. By balancing persistence with respect, tailoring content to the audience, and varying interaction types, the sales team can stay top of mind without overwhelming or annoying prospects.

Thoughtful, data-driven content scheduling and strategic engagement ensure that the social sales strategy builds long-term relationships and drives meaningful results.

References:

1. https://www.contentgrip.com/why-is-consistency-in-content-marketing-important
2. https://www.linkedin.com/advice/0/whats-best-way-persistent-without-being-annoying-c9txc
3. https://buffer.com/resources/best-time-to-post-on-linkedin/
4. https://www.linkedin.com/pulse/personalized-prospecting-compliment-your-prospects-brandon-bornancin

CONCLUSION

Start Simple And Build Over Time

The Key Takeaways

To start building a B2B social sales strategy, the first step is identifying the target audience and understanding their needs, challenges, and preferred platforms. Developing a strong personal and brand presence on those platforms is essential, which involves optimizing profiles and sharing relevant, valuable content.

Establishing connections with key decision-makers and nurturing these relationships through consistent, tailored communication is another critical step. Utilizing social listening tools to monitor conversations and track engagement helps refine the approach.

Finally, aligning the strategy with marketing efforts ensures a cohesive message and maximizes outreach potential, setting the foundation for long-term success.

You made it to the end! This is the final chapter and here I really just want to give some ideas and tips on the next steps. I have shared a lot of information in this book and now I want to help you build a roadmap that can guide you into the future.

Building a successful B2B social sales strategy involves several key components, but the most important aspects can be broken down into manageable steps that allow even a time-poor manager to get started without feeling overwhelmed. Here's a summary of the core elements and some practical "baby steps" to get started on implementing the strategy:

Key Aspects of a B2B Social Sales Strategy:

1. **Consistency and Presence:**
    - Maintaining a regular and authentic presence on social media platforms is critical. This helps build trust, stay top of mind, and demonstrate expertise.
    - It's about being visible without being overbearing, delivering value rather than pushing sales too hard.

2. **Defining the Ideal Customer Profile (ICP):**
    - Understanding your target audience's pain points, needs, and challenges is essential for creating relevant content and engaging effectively.

- Tailor your outreach and content to fit your prospects' interests, positioning yourself as a problem-solver, not just a seller.

2. **Content Strategy:**
    - High-quality, relevant content that addresses the pain points of your target audience is vital. Use a mix of blogs, whitepapers, case studies, videos, and infographics.
    - Content should provide value, offer insights, and establish your team as thought leaders in the industry.

4. **Engagement and Interaction:**
    - Actively engaging with prospects, influencers, and industry experts by commenting on posts, participating in discussions, and sharing relevant content helps build relationships and trust.
    - Prompt, meaningful interactions show prospects that you're invested in the relationship.

5. **Social Listening:**
    - Monitoring social platforms for mentions of your company, competitors, and industry trends allows you to understand your audience better, identify opportunities, and respond proactively.
    - Use social listening tools to gather insights and engage strategically.

6. **Network Building:**
   - Focus on building connections with prospects and influencers on platforms like LinkedIn.
   - Participate in virtual industry events, webinars, and forums to expand your reach and demonstrate your expertise in the field.

7. **Value Proposition and Personalization:**
   - Clearly communicate your product's or service's unique value in a way that addresses the specific needs of each prospect.
   - Personalize outreach so that your message feels tailored, making it less salesy and more relevant.

8. **Measuring Success:**
   - Use analytics tools to track the performance of your social activities and content.
   - Set clear goals and KPIs for lead generation, engagement, and conversion, but avoid getting stuck on vanity metrics—focus on actual business results, like conversions and pipeline growth.

How to Get Started Without Feeling Overwhelmed:

This is the reality for most executives. If your job is building a sales pipeline and you have a target on your back then building a content strategy can feel like too much effort.

But this is an essential process. Smart companies will have some support for the sales team - this may even be managed in partnership with the marketing team. Some will work with a ghostwriter so the ideas and topics can be formulated by your sales team, but they can then allow a professional writer to create some polished blogs that can then be used in the name of your team.

For time-poor managers, it's easy to feel like there's too much to do. Here are some manageable steps to start building a social sales strategy without being overwhelmed:

1. **Define Your Goals and Audience (Small but Crucial First Step)**
    - Start by setting a few clear, realistic goals. What do you want to achieve in your first 6 months? Lead generation? Brand awareness? Thought leadership?
    - Define your target audience or ideal customer profile (ICP) based on current clients and industry trends. Focus on understanding their pain points and needs. This will inform your content and engagement.

2. **Focus on One Platform to Start (e.g., LinkedIn)**
    - Don't try to be everywhere at once. Pick one social platform that's most relevant to your business (for most B2B, this is LinkedIn).
    - Set up your LinkedIn profile (or those of key sales execs) to clearly reflect expertise, thought leadership, and the company's unique value proposition.

3. **Create a Simple Content Plan (Baby Steps)**
    - Develop a very basic content calendar for the first month. You don't need to post every day—start with 2–3 posts per week.

- Share curated industry news, a customer success story, or a short blog post. Focus on being consistent rather than trying to be everywhere at once.

4. **Start Engaging (Comment, Like, and Share)**
   - Begin by commenting thoughtfully on posts from industry influencers and key prospects. This allows you to engage without the pressure of creating your own content right away.
   - Share relevant articles or insights from others in your field to stay visible without needing to create content constantly. This is simple if you are just focused on LinkedIn… just click the 'Share to LinkedIn' button when you read something interesting in the news and add a sentence or two to add your own thoughts.

5. **Use Social Listening Tools for Insights (Simplify with Tools)**
   - Use a social listening tool (or even LinkedIn notifications) to monitor what's happening in your industry and keep track of mentions of your brand or competitors.
   - This helps you find engagement opportunities without having to manually monitor everything.

6. **Measure Small Wins (Don't Overcomplicate Metrics)**
   - Instead of getting lost in analytics, focus on small wins like an increase in engagement on

your posts, new connections, or a valuable conversation started.

- As you get more comfortable, you can start tracking more sophisticated KPIs, like lead conversions or pipeline growth.

7. **Delegate Where Possible (Involve the Team)**
    - If possible, delegate aspects of the strategy to team members. For example, marketing can handle content creation while sales focuses on relationship building and engagement.
    - Use social media management tools to schedule posts and streamline the process.

8. **Consistent Presence, Not Overposting (Balance)**
    - Focus on maintaining a regular, visible presence without over-posting. Quality and relevance are more important than volume.
    - Over time, this will help build your credibility without overwhelming your audience.
    - Sharing one of two news stories daily is more than enough and if you are creating your own original content - such as blogs - then weekly is a good rhythm.

Starting Simple, Building Over Time

The key to starting a B2B social sales strategy without feeling overwhelmed is to break it down into manageable, actionable steps.

Begin by focusing on one platform, defining your audience, and creating a simple content plan. Consistently engage with prospects and influencers, measure small wins, and gradually build out your strategy as you become more comfortable.

By starting small and staying focused on quality and consistency, even the busiest managers can implement a successful social sales strategy that builds relationships and drives results over time.

Slow and steady can win. The great thing about strategic content is that it does live on. Paul O'Hara wrote the foreword to this book. Go and look at his LinkedIn profile and explore all the articles he has written - there are hundreds going back over a decade.

Even his first article lives on and this consistency itself sends a message to anyone searching for his details online. This is someone with ideas, with an opinion, and with insight.

Maybe this is someone I should call when I need advice in his area of expertise?

THE SOCIAL SALES PLAYBOOK:

Developing a B2B Sales Plan That Drives Results

APPENDIX

Driving Into A New Future For B2B Social Sales

Relationships have always been important in the business to consumer (B2C) sales environment. Brands endlessly advertise a lifestyle, rather than the value of the product they are actually offering. They want to become a part of your life, rather than just the cold drink you need on a hot day.

Why isn't B2B relationship-building seen the same way?

B2B relationships do exist, but it's only recently that the idea of social sales for B2B brands has been taken more seriously.

A social approach to B2B sales allows the vendor to build a rapport with potential clients - as well as influencers who may promote their services. It's the opposite of cold calls or emails, because there is something actively worth discussing.

This relationship building is becoming critically important in the customer experience (CX) and business process outsourcing (BPO) environment - for a good reason.

Hiring a company to manage your CX is not a one-time purchase. It's not like ordering a laptop, or photocopier, or box of post-it notes. When a company hires a CX specialist, that service provider will soon become the public face of the brand. The employees of the service provider will be answering the phone, texts, and emails and replying as if they represent the client. That's a big responsibility.

Traditionally the RFP process has been used to select partners - create a shortlist of potential CX specialists and then compare their responses to an RFP. However, there are many signs that this approach is becoming dated because it tends to focus on very specific metrics, such as the contract value, rather than the outcomes desired from the relationship - such as increasing customer lifetime value.

The only way that a CX specialist can bypass the RFP process is by building a trusted relationship with potential partners to the point that when the company needs help, they turn to the specialist they already trust.

This often happens when an executive leaves one company and moves to another. They often call on the suppliers they know rather than starting a lengthy RFP process that will compare suppliers more systematically. In some cases, the RFP is unavoidable, such as public procurement, but a trusted supplier does have a head start.

So how does an active social sales policy help to build trust? There are a number of ways, but imagine if you are a CX specialist today in 2024 and you started using content on a platform like LinkedIn - what can you achieve quickly?

Conversations with prospects: think about who is on your prospect list. What problems are they facing? Can you write about the type of problems they face and use a prospect as an example of a company facing these challenges - and how best to handle the situation? When your article is published, it's a lot easier to send it to them or tag them on LinkedIn so a conversation is started - discussing an industry problem is a lot better than a cold call.

Assurance to clients: your content platform allows you to also highlight some of the wins that your clients have achieved. They were smart to choose your company so why not highlight exactly how smart and massage their ego a little at the same time? Demonstrate success.

Exploring Innovation: demonstrate that you can see what is coming down the track by exploring new ideas and thought leadership. If a company is thinking about how they will manage CX in a new environment then have you already written content exploring those issues? Companies hire a CX specialist to manage the day-to-day interactions, but they also want to see that you know what may happen next year. Are you a real expert?

Engaging with analysts: analysts are always looking for new ideas and services so if you have an interesting story to tell then grab the attention of the analyst community by looking at what they have been publishing recently and commenting on it. I once helped a client of mine to create a blog saying that the annual conference of a major analyst was missing some of the biggest topics in CX that year - he was invited to join the event and deliver a keynote speech.

Media coverage: the media is always covering CX, but often without much insight. However, it is the business press and serious news journals where most executives get their news. If you see a ridiculous business story such as the Washington Post saying all CX jobs are being immediately replaced by AI then write a response. Get your voice published with information from inside the industry. Tag the journalist - maybe the next time they want to write about CX they will call you for a quote.

These are just a few ideas - scratching the surface. There are many other networks - especially visual ones like TikTok and Instagram. However, LinkedIn is often a focus for business executives. People buy from people, even in the B2B environment, so sales leaders need to be visible. They need to demonstrate their expertise and carefully use content to start conversations with the influencers or prospects that can help their business.

I published a book on executive blogging nine years ago. It has been clear to me for a long time that content can be very influential in nurturing B2B relationships. I'm in the process of revising a new version of that old book that will include several entirely new sections on B2B social sales and content.

In an era of increasing B2B relationships and the changing B2B buying process I think this book could be an extremely valuable summary of what really matters for B2B sales in 2024.

Originally published on LinkedIn on January 3, 2024. Follow this link to access the article: bit.ly/drivinginto

Mark Hillary

Do you need a ghostwriter to help you make some of this a reality? Follow this link and we can talk about building a blogging strategy even if your team has no time to write or create content…

www.markhillary.com

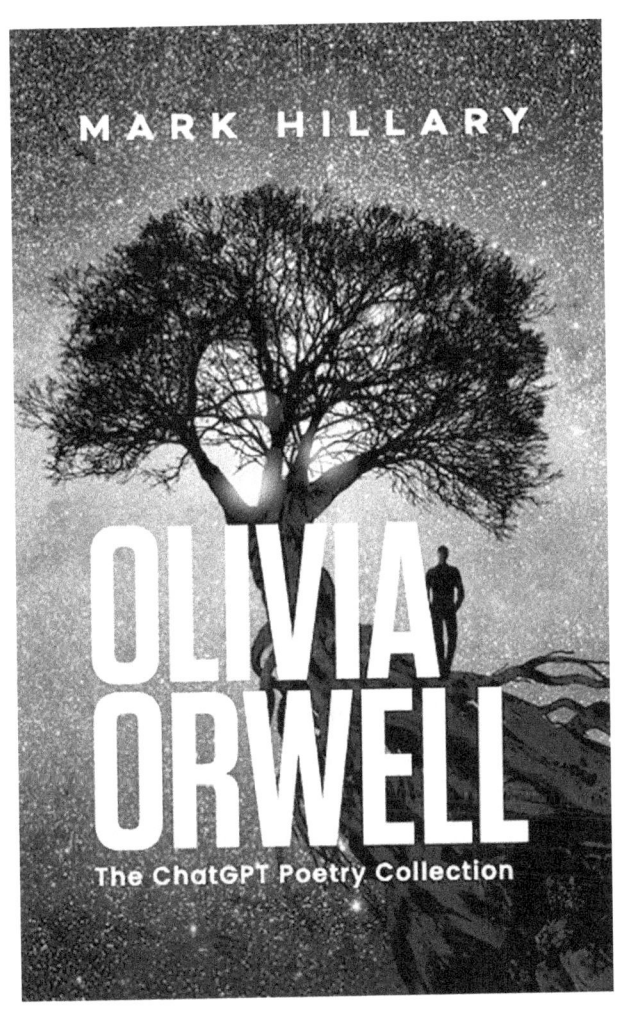

Also by Mark Hillary

The Social Sales Playbook:
Developing a B2B Sales Plan That Drives Results

by

Mark Hillary

© Mark Hillary 2024
All Rights Reserved

Published by Carnaby Books
São Paulo, Brazil

www.carnabysp.com
www.markhillary.com

www.ingramcontent.com/pod-product-compliance
Lightning Source LLC
Chambersburg PA
CBHW052153220526
45471CB00004B/1656